MY TWENTIETH CENTURY

ALSO BY DAVID KIRBY

POETRY

THE OPERA LOVER
SARAH BERNHARDT'S LEG
SAVING THE YOUNG MEN OF VIENNA
BIG-LEG MUSIC *(an Orchises book)*

LITERARY CRITICISM

INDIVIDUAL AND COMMUNITY: VARIATIONS ON A THEME
IN AMERICAN FICTION *(with Kenneth H. Baldwin)*
AMERICAN FICTION TO 1900:
A GUIDE TO INFORMATION SOURCES
GRACE KING
AMERICA'S HIVE OF MONEY: FOREIGN SOURCES OF AMERICAN FICTION
THROUGH HENRY JAMES
THE SUN RISES IN THE EVENING:
MONISM AND QUIETISM IN WESTERN CULTURE
THE PLURAL WORLD: AN INTERDISCIPLINARY GLOSSARY
OF CONTEMPORARY AMERICAN THOUGHT
MARK STRAND AND THE POET'S PLACE IN CONTEMPORARY CULTURE
THE PORTRAIT OF A LADY AND THE TURN OF THE SCREW:
HENRY JAMES AND MELODRAMA
BOYISHNESS IN AMERICAN CULTURE
HERMAN MELVILLE

TEXTBOOK

WRITING POETRY:
WHERE POEMS COME FROM AND HOW TO WRITE THEM

FOR CHILDREN

THE COWS ARE GOING TO PARIS *(with Allen Woodman)*
THE BEAR WHO CAME TO STAY *(with Allen Woodman)*

MY TWENTIETH CENTURY

poems

DAVID KIRBY

ORCHISES
WASHINGTON
1999

Library of Congress Cataloging in Publication Data

Kirby, David K.
My twentieth century / poems / David Kirby.
   p. cm.
ISBN 0-914061-76-3 (alk. paper)
   I. Title.
PS3561.I66M96   1999
811'.54—dc20   98-12928
                                                          CIP

ACKNOWLEDGEMENTS

Versions of the following poems appeared for the first time in these magazines:

Apalachee Quarterly: "Mr. Andrews"; *Chicago Review:* "The Afterlife," "Something Wild"; *Denver Quarterly:* "W. C. Rice's Cross Garden"; *Five Points:* "The Ghost of Henry James"; *Kenyon Review:* "Summer of the Cuban Missile Crisis"; *Mississippi Review:* "Sex Therapy"; *New Orleans Review:* "Crying," "Laughing"; *North Dakota Quarterly:* "Sacred Monsters"; *Northwest Quarterly:* "The Big Jacket," "My Twentieth Century"; *Parnassus:* "Polio"; *Ploughshares:* "Lurch, Whose Story Never Ends"; *River Styx:* "Electricity," "Neighbors"; *Southern Review:* "Listening to John Crowe Ransom Read His Poetry," "The Money Changer," "A Really Good Story."

A version of "The King is Dead" appeared first in *Isle of Flowers: Poems by Florida's Individual Artist Fellows,* ed. Donna J. Long, Helen Pruitt Wallace, and Rick Campbell (Tallahassee, Florida: Anhinga Press, 1995).

Versions of the following poems appeared first in *Big-Leg Music* (Washington, D.C.: Orchises, 1995): "Lurch, Whose Story Doesn't End," "The Money Changer," and "The Summer of the Cuban Missile Crisis."

An essay based on the incidents recounted in "Mr. Andrews" appeared as "Some Lessons on Labor From a Boss of Few Words" in *The New York Times,* September 3, 1995, F-11.

Thanks to the Florida Arts Council for a grant which made this work possible.

And lavish thanks to Barbara Hamby for reading these particular poems, sure, but mainly for talking about poetry with me day and night, in cars and bars and metro stops, during the last days of the twentieth century. "Come to the window, sweet is the night-air!"

Manufactured in the United States of America

Orchises Press
P. O. Box 20602
Alexandria
Virginia
22320-1602

G6E4C2A

TABLE OF CONTENTS

To Their Serene Majesties,

The Years January 1, 1900-November 28, 1944

Weather's beautiful—wish you were here.

Love,

Do not applaud. It is not I who speak,
but history which speaks through me.

—Fustel de Coulanges
on entering a lecture hall to the applause of students

Author's Note

As I begin thinking about these new poems,
I am invited to give a reading
   at a conference in Fairhope, Alabama
and only when I get there do I find out
   that I am not some kind of featured reader
who is going to be paid a reasonable fee
   and expenses but a mere conference participant
like everyone else, all of whom, it seems,
   have been invited to give readings.

And since I had just got $600 the week before
for a presentation in Hattiesburg, Mississippi,
   I am sitting there listening to someone else read,
someone not nearly as good as I am,
   and thinking, Stinks, this really stinks,
and I am brooding and feeling sorry for myself
   and reading the conference program over and over
the way one does in hopes of finding something
   of even mild interest on the thirty-ninth

or fortieth perusal, even though it isn't there
the first thirty-eight times, and suddenly
   I see, "3:00: Ted Solotaroff. Reception Hall,"
and I think, Ted Solotaroff? *The* Ted Solotaroff?
   The Ted Solotaroff who founded *New American Review,*
which for years was one of the best magazines around
   and which I used as a text in more than one
of my classes, and was also a senior editor
   at Harper & Row and is a celebrated essayist himself?

Must be some other Ted Solotaroff, I think,
since the real one wouldn't be at this crummy conference,
   although later I find out that he is spending a year
as a visiting professor at the university
   in Tuscaloosa, only two hours away, which means
it would actually be desirable for him to hop down
   to Fairhope, which is a rather picturesque

9

little town once you get over the self-pity,
  especially considering he is probably getting paid

  to appear, which I am not.
But I forget all this when Mr. Solotaroff
  begins to speak: his talk is called
"A Few Good Voices in My Head,"
  and in it he refers to an essay by Walter Benjamin—
"my main man," as Mr. Solotaroff calls him—
  entitled "The Storyteller," which appears
in Benjamin's first book, *Illuminations,*
  and which deals with the dying art of storytelling.

  By now I'm almost crawling into Mr. Solotaroff's lap,
of course, because storytelling is exactly
  what I want to do in these new poems I'm writing,
and if storytelling is dying or if it has already died
  (and Benjamin said it died after World War I),
then I don't know whether to be sad that there is
  no market for this new passion of mine or overjoyed,
because if all my competitors have been dead for
  seventy-five years, then I've got the monopoly.

                    * * *

  So when Mr. Solotaroff finishes his talk,
I rush up and shake his hand with both of mine
  and make sure I get the titles of both essays right
and say goodbye to the people who invited me
  and whine a little bit more about not getting paid—
but not too much, because I am almost beside myself
  with my own emotions, and I rush back to Tallahassee
and go straight to the library and get *Illuminations*
  and start reading it at the stoplights

  on the way home, and the first thing I read is,
"Boredom is the dream bird that hatches the egg
  of experience," and then this sentence
about the effect of World War I on the men
  who had fought it: "A generation that had gone

to school on a horse-drawn streetcar now stood
  under the open sky in a countryside in which
nothing remained unchanged but the clouds,"
  and by now I'm nearly passing out,

    because who says all the great lines
are only in poems and plays and novels? And while
  I was at the library getting *Illuminations,*
I also got Mr. Solotaroff's collection, the title
  of which is the same as the essay he read in Fairhope,
so that when I am finally back in my house,
  I start in on it as well, not even unpacking
but reading a little of the one essay and then
  a little of the other, the way you might stand

    at a buffet table and eat a mouthful of cheese
and follow that with a few grapes and then
  some cheese again, cheese and grapes, grapes
and cheese, thus more than doubling your pleasure
  because the two tastes in alternation somehow amount
to a third. And what I learn from these two essayists
  together is, as Mr. Solotaroff puts it, that a piece
of writing is often a writer's "only way to organize
    and *to some extent* comprehend life's fullness

    and perplexity" (emphasis mine), which is
exactly what I need to hear, because
  for the past several months, I've been working
on what I call "memory poems" or longish narrative poems
  that stick as closely as possible to events
I actually experienced. Each memory poem
  is thus part poem / part memoir, though each
has a certain shape to it that mere autobiography
    doesn't have, because even if the events

    are exactly as I remember them, I realize
that they have been tumbled in the mind enough
  to have acquired a kind of symmetry,
with certain figures looming large—
  it's like after you walk around in Rome, say,

and what you remember later are all the statues.
   As to where the events come from, that's easy:
these are the stories I used to dine out on,
   the ones I'd tell, not one or two but fifty

   or a hundred times, because obviously there was
something in them that to my mind bore retelling,
   and occasionally people would even ask for, say,
the one about the crazy babysitter or the man
   I worked for one summer who only spoke to me
twice. I used to tell my students they ought
   to kick themselves if they haven't made poems out of
the stories they tell their friends, so now
   it looks as though it's my turn to bend over.

* * *

   Like everybody, I write in the manner of my masters,
although the nice thing about being a slave to the arts
   is that you get to change masters from time to time.
Besides, what I mean by "master" in this case
   is not so much someone you imitate as someone
who is like a little household god you look up to
   and who sort of stands behind you whenever you need
somebody to back you up—someone about whom you can say,
   as Gorky did of Tolstoy, "As long as this man is alive,

   I am not alone in the world." Anyway, whereas
I started out being influenced by Emily Dickinson
   and Gerard Manley Hopkins and writing in that sort
of metaphysical way that many poets still like,
   it wasn't long before I used Whitman and Ginsberg
to help me become more dithyrambic and prophetic—
   I mean, I sounded or at least I tried to sound
like a prophet, not that I went around predicting
   the imminent arrival of tall handsome strangers—

   and then used poets as different
as Frank O'Hara and Caroline Knox and Christy Sanford
   to help me write a breathy, witty, poem

that tried to be "smart" in every sense of the word.
    At the moment, I don't know that very many other poets
are writing exactly the way I am right now,
    but certainly David Antin's work is close
to what I'm doing here, even though his poems
    are even longer and more diffuse than mine,

    and the same with Spalding Gray's monologues,
which are longer still yet more compact
    than Antin's poems though not mine, and the same again
with the spoken pieces performed by Henry Rollins,
    who used to front the punk band Black Flag but now
tours the country telling stories closer in content
    to my work than either Antin's or Gray's,
even if they are less literary, at least
    in the traditional sense, than either of theirs.

    And as I put together my new idea of what
it was that I wanted to do, I also had in mind
    the cartoons of Stan Mack that used to appear in
The Village Voice, little street vignettes that
    always begin with a tag line that says, "Guaranteed:
All Dialogue Reported Verbatim." To promise
    to limit oneself strictly to what had
actually happened: this could be
    tremendously liberating, I thought.

    The only problem is that now
I don't have those stories to tell at dinner,
    but then things keep happening to me.
That's the great thing about stories,
    that there's no end to them.
But now I have to guard against either trying
    to make things happen so I can write about them
or trying to write about them
    while they're still happening,

    and sometimes I feel like a peanut seller
at a ball game, frozen in mid-transaction
    as the big play unfolds; I've got a bag

of nuts in one hand and somebody's change
  in the other, yet my eyes are on the field.
But at least I'm there;
  I didn't hear the game on the radio.
Because if I write about it,
    and you read what I've written, it happened.

Baton Rouge-Baltimore-Tallahassee-Florence-Paris
November 29, 1944-November 29, 1997

Polio

Our mothers were so afraid
that they wouldn't even let us take the bus,
    because in those days, nobody had the slightest idea
how polio was transmitted. I caught it anyway.
    Nobody knows how, and it doesn't really matter,
although my mother used to grumble about
    a neighbor of ours, a doctor with a lot of nutty ideas
who had an unfiltered swimming pool in his back yard,
    a scummy green pond, really, where we kids
used to swim. In the beginning, I fell a lot,
    but I was five years old then, and my parents
attributed the falls to a child's clumsiness.

Then one day I was going down the steps
and my legs gave way and I went off one side
    and rolled over in the dirt a couple of times
and looked up and saw my mother watching me
    with a worried look, and even I, who was only five,
thought, This isn't right, and the next thing
    I knew, I was sitting in Dr. Van Gelder's office,
and the next thing after that, I was being checked into
    Baton Rouge General, where I spent the next three
and a half months. I turned six in the hospital
    and had this crummy birthday party with paper hats
and a lot of forced gaiety on the part of the nurses

    and none at all on the part of the other kids,
with whom I had nothing in common except
    a crippling disease and the desire to get the hell out.
And then there was Christmas, which was more of the same,
    and New Year's Eve, when my father stayed late,
right up till they shooed him away, whereupon he kissed me
    and said, See you next year! which is a funny joke
of the kind fathers are fond of. And I knew
    what he meant, too, only I didn't. Did and didn't,
did and didn't, until finally I dragged myself
    out of bed and over to the window,
where I looked down on the parking lot,

which was nearly empty, and saw my father
come out of the building and walk through
    the yellow pools of light in his long winter coat
and his 1950s dad-style felt hat until he reached
    our big four-hole Buick, which he got into
and drove away, and I thought, Well,
    that's the last I'll see of my dad for a year,
and I threw my head back and howled like a wolf cub,
    and the other little cripples in the polio ward
turned uneasily and went right on sleeping
    as waves of self-pity built and broke over me
and drove me back to my bed, where, at last, I too slept.

    Now that was strange: not the failed joke
or my going to the window, but the sleep of the others,
    because every night we got up after Lights Out
and jumped around in our beds and acted silly,
    and if some of the kids were already sleeping,
the rest would go around in their little hospital gowns
    and wake the sleepers, and pretty soon
we'd all be flopping around in our beds like catfish.
    We'd do flips, knee drops, back layouts,
the whole gymnastic repertoire. It wasn't pretty,
    and I wonder that it didn't set back our progress
and even leave us crippled for life,

    since the nurses were always threatening us
and saying we'd lie still if we knew
    what was good for us, but then I also thought
maybe the doctors knew how fidgety kids are
    and therefore took our foolishness into account
when they designed our whole program,
    in which case the nurses were trying to get us
to be quiet not because exercise was wrong
    but so they wouldn't be bothered, and here
I'm thinking of this one nurse in particular
    who slapped me once after I threw up in bed
and then pressed my call button

as they'd taught us to do if we needed anything,
so I pressed it, and the next thing I knew,
    pow, right across the chops—not especially
humane treatment for a kid, even a well one,
        because a kid's stomach holds about as much as,
what, a soup bowl, I'd say, and the distance
    from its stomach to its mouth is maybe six inches,
and that's why kids are always throwing up.
        But this was back when any adult had the right
to discipline any child, theirs or someone else's,
    so how was I to know I was getting a raw deal?
I just figured, Oh, well, life in the polio ward.

    We did a lot of therapy in that ward:
walking between handrails, pulling the levers
    of various machines, and stretching,
which was the worst, on account of my muscles
        being like bunched-up steel coils instead of
long, supple ropes. The therapist would have me
    sit spread-legged and reach for a nickel
she'd placed between my knees, and I'd lean forward
        about a sixteenth of an inch and yelp with pain
and rest and lean forward a little bit more
    until finally I'd either pick up the nickel
or complain so much that they had to give it to me,

        and on a good day I'd even get a Payday candy bar
as an extra reward or extra bribe to be quiet,
    the Payday being nougat rolled in salted peanuts
and my absolutely favorite bar to this day.
        We also did a lot of hydrotherapy, which was
less fun than it sounds, because the pool
    was big and noisy, and I was little and weak
and hadn't learned to swim yet. Hydrotherapy
        followed breakfast, a meal I've never skipped,
and this one morning I remember having french toast,
    which, like all six-year-olds, with or without polio,
I drenched in an excess of syrup.

I was already feeling a little rocky
when the orderly came for me,
    and after fifteen minutes of being parboiled
in those roiling waters, I was ready to heave,
    which is when the orderly hoisted me out
and wrapped me in my terrycloth robe.
    Whheeerrrch! Out came the french toast,
all over the orderly's shoulders and down his back.
    Now this guy had serious muscles;
he was one of those characters who looked
    as though doctors had surgically implanted
golf balls and Irish potatoes under his coppery skin,

    and I figured, This could be it,
this could be the big one right here,
    especially remembering the nurse
who had slapped me for throwing up in bed
    just a couple of weeks earlier,
so I huddled against the guy's monster chest
    and shook like the coward I'd every right to be
and waited for him to throw me against the wall.
    But instead he patted my back and said,
There, there, baby, there, there,
    until the spasms subsided and I realized
he wasn't going to murder me after all.

    Then February came, and I was discharged.
I had to go to the Ochsner Clinic in New Orleans
    for semi-annual and then annual checkups,
but that wasn't so bad, because afterwards
    my parents took me to Commander's Palace
for Trout Almandine and Meringue Glacée,
    and also because I liked my New Orleans physician,
Doctor St. Ives, who had jet-black hair
    and glossy red lips and a Jane Russell figure
that her lab coat didn't disguise,
    which was something I appreciated more and more
as I turned ten and eleven and then twelve.

I recovered almost completely and could play
any sport I wanted to, which didn't mean
    I was any good at it; I played football,
for example, but I was only second-string
    and I barely lettered my senior year.
Yet gradually polio became a dim memory for me,
    and I only came to think of it at odd moments,
as, for example, after JFK was shot
    and there were all those suspicious deaths
involving people associated, however obliquely,
    with the investigation, including Doctor St. Ives,
who was beaten to death with a hammer

    by an unknown assailant and who had worked
on a cancer project with David Ferry,
    thought by many to be the go-between for Oswald
and the money men who were backing him.
    Or once I was in London to talk with an editor
who was my age and whom I had never seen
    face to face, and when I walked in, he heaved
himself up on his crutches and smiled and said,
    Don't mind me, I had polio in the Great Epidemic,
and before I could stop myself, I said, Me, too,
    and he cocked his head and pinched his brows
into an expression that said, Liar.

    But otherwise, it was no big deal,
and in one sense my polio affected my parents
    more than it did me, saddening their marriage
so much that it was years before
    they could figure out how to be happy together
the way they were before I got sick.
    In fact, I think a lot of people
don't believe me when I say I had polio
    because I don't fit their stereotype of someone
all twisted up like a pretzel.
    If I have to, or if I've had a drink too many,
sometimes I lower my trousers and say,

Look, see how my left thigh
is a little smaller than my right?
    And they'll say, Oh, yeah, sorry,
but I don't do it that often because,
        after all, maybe I just have one smaller leg
and also maybe they ought to take my word for it
    in the first place. And sometimes I'll go over
to the university in a pair of shorts,
        and some overanxious grad student
or one of those guys from the German Department
    will get right up in my face and say,
Ha! You've got skinny legs! and smile

    to show me that we're such great buddies
he can insult me, and I just say something like,
    Yup, legs like these never go out of style,
because why get into it with that kind of person?
    Yet I'll say this: I'm all for the monkeys, too,
but those animal-rights fanatics ought to be glad
    they're healthy enough to walk a picket line;
I remember crawling past this row of iron lungs
    I'd see lined up in the hospital corridor,
the people inside them looking at their lives
    through a rear-view mirror because nobody
had come up with a vaccine in time for them.

    The heroes of the Great Epidemic were Doctors Salk,
who developed the injectable vaccine in 1952,
    and Sabin, who came up with the oral version
seven years later—both a little late for me,
    but as I say, I wasn't hit that hard.
Besides, my personal hero is the nameless orderly
    who calmly went about his duty after I threw up
all over him, and sometimes I'm startled to find myself
    thinking of his example, both as a guy
who did what he was paid to do, no matter how awful,
    and also as a human being who saw his chance
to be nasty to someone and didn't take it.

    He was quite possibly the most fully-evolved person
I've ever met, because on the surface most people

are pretty decent, pretty agreeable, and that's the way
most of them are most of the time, so no problem.
    And then below that surface decency there is a core
of savagery running almost all the way to the center—
    like, within a nanometer of our best hearts—
and a fraction of the race has got that far,
    which is too bad for the rest of us. But after that
it's like the Garden of Eden in there—or the Elysian Fields,
    maybe, and I don't mean the boulevard in Paris, either,
but a holy place, the abode of the blessed.

The King Is Dead

The woman who hands me my dry cleaning
   is red-eyed and red-faced, and I think, Jeez,
she's going to hurt herself
  if she doesn't stop trying so hard not to cry,
so I say, "Hold on, it can't be that bad,"
   and she drops my slacks and blazer

on the counter and puts her hands
  over her face and says, "Oh, boo-hoo! BOO-HOO!
The kang is dead, the kang is dead!"
   and the woman behind her
looks at me and silently mouths the word, "Elvis,"

and I, God help me, say, "So?" to myself,
   or at least I hope it was to myself,
because I don't like to hurt people's feelings,
  but Elvis had always seemed like
the biggest fake in the world to me:
   my racist cousins who lived in the sticks

would sob their mascara off every time
  an Elvis song came on the radio,
but I figured, Forget it: the only good music
   was not the music Elvis made but the music
Elvis listened to and then watered down

so that white people could stand to be around it,
   and here I'm referring to the kinds of songs
being sung at the same time by Rufus Thomas,
  Irma Thomas, Carla Thomas, Otis Redding,
Barrett Strong, and Doris Troy. Chuck Berry.
   Little Richard. Aretha Franklin. Fontella Bass.

Elvis had already lost me in December 1954
  with that false start to "Milkcow Blues Boogie"
("Hold it, fellas. That don't move. Let's get
   real, real gone"); besides, Georges Braque
said that in art there is only one thing

that counts, the thing you can't explain,
    and there was nothing you couldn't explain
about Elvis. Also, anybody who had the Jordanaires
    for a back-up group. . . . Meanwhile,
what about Rufus, Irma, Carla and company?
    Item: I am sitting in the breakfast room of a hotel

in Colmar, in France, having come to see
    the Isenheim Altarpiece of Matthias Grünewald,
and as I break and butter my roll,
    "Good Golly Miss Molly" comes on the radio,
and the most staid Germans, the most dour Swedes,

the most cynical French smile and wiggle
    their shoulders and sort of bop their coffee cups
around their saucers as Richard makes them
    ting-a-ling-a-ling, good golly! Sure like to ball!
Item: in the bootheel of Italy, I am walking out
    of the castle of Otranto (yes, there really is one,

though Horace Walpole never saw it) and hear
    James Brown singing it's a man's world and he's LOST!
in the wilderness and he's LOST! in the emptiness,
    and I glance sideways to see that, like me,
my fellow travelers are LOST! in those big chords,

jerking to a halt every time they get LOST!
    and then almost crawling through the heat and the sun
until the next time their spines stiffen and
    they're LOST! in the song and in James Brown's voice,
because, yes, rhythm and blues is like Deutschland,
    it's über alles, whereas Elvis would be a dim memory

to most people were it not for the *Weekly World News*
    and those crappy oldie stations that people listen to
so they can find out what they missed
    back when they were too busy painting signs for
their pro-segregation rallies to listen to the radio.

But my personal favorites always were
   and always will be the crooners and balladeers,
the great soul men in their jewelry and shiny suits:
  Mr. Solomon Burke, Mr. Chuck Jackson, Mr. Bobby Bland,
Mr. Jerry Butler, Mr. Tyrone Davis (whom I spent
   forty dollars to see once, even though he did

a ten-minute set and said, "Thank you very much,
  you've been wonderful"), and, above these and every other,
the real king, the one and only, the late great
    Mr. Sam Cooke. These gentlemen were way beyond cool.
Also, they had what I wanted. No, not women: audiences.

They also had that pomade, that just-pressed
   white shirt, those syrupy phrasings,
that lush orchestration—those violin
  and horn sections—yet these were like
the candy shell for something else,
   something that had no name, though you'd know it

when you tasted it because it would race
  through your veins and into your skull like a brush fire,
whatever it was, and the flames of Hell
   would leap up where your brain used to be,
and you'd like it and you'd know what Kant meant

when he said that the sublime is better
   than the merely beautiful because it hurts.
And I am not talking about carnal desire;
 I am talking about what cannot be talked about,
as, for example, in the dreamboat mise-en-scène
    Sam Cooke describes in "We're Having a Party."

The cokes are in the icebox, the popcorn's
  on the table, the guy and his girl
are dancing to the radio—you know it can't last.
   There's more to come, though you don't know what it is,
just as you can hear more in the slight roughness

of Sam Cooke's buttered-popcorn voice
   in the January 12, 1963 live session
at the Harlem Square Club in North Miami.
  Just think, JFK was still alive then
and good-looking, too. He was just as handsome
    as Sam Cooke. He was just as ingenuous

as the rest of us, thinking things would go on
  as they always had: touch football
in the front yard, a clean little war here and there,
    some side action in the old sex department
but nothing for anyone to get upset about,

and all the while the economy just keeps on
    inching forward. And then it's November 22,
and the limo swings slowly around the corner,
  and, rip, suddenly there's a big seam
right down the middle of history:
    everybody starts locking their doors

at night, trick-or-treaters don't go out
  without their parents, and at least
one clean little war grows into a dirty big one
    and then fragments into a dozen
dirty little ones that never seem to end.

A year later, Sam Cooke, wearing only a sports coat
    and a pair of shoes, is shot to death
by the manager of a three-dollar-a-night motel;
  more than 200,000 people view his body,
and at his funeral Ray Charles sings a song
    called "Angels Keep Watching Over Me." Sam Cooke

sang like an angel. Sam Cooke makes me think
  of Herman Melville. Sometimes when I hear
Sam Cooke's voice I feel as though I'm "speeding up,"
    as Robert Lowell used to say when he started to go
into one of his manic phases,

and that's when I feel about soul music what
    James Dickey must have felt about poetry when he said
it was "just naturally the greatest goddamn thing
  that ever was in the whole universe." Sometimes
I go out in the morning, and it is raining so hard
    that the vines seem ready to reach up out of the earth

and pull me down and drown me. And on other days
  the sun is out, and I still have the taste of a great cup
of coffee in my mouth, and there's already a hint of fall
    in the air, and my team won the night before,
and Sam Cooke is still dead.

The Summer of the Cuban Missile Crisis

Dickie asked if we were hungry, and Art and I
  said yeah, sure, so he pulled into the Walt Whitman
Service Plaza near Camden and there, in front
  of the very Howard Johnson's where we planned to eat,
was a bus with painted fire blazing down its sides
  and above it, in letters two feet high, the words
JAMES BROWN AND THE FAMOUS FLAMES, and I thought,
  righhht, this is it: I am sixteen years old,

I have my first paying job, I'm traveling across country
  with two guys who are older and cooler than I am
yet who seem to accept me as their equal,
  and now I'm going to meet Mr. I Got You, Mr. Get Up
(I Feel Like Being A) Sex Machine, Mr. I Break Out
  in a Cold Sweat, the Hardest Working Man
in Show Business, James Brown himself.

Dickie was Dickie Biles, and Art was Arthur Kennedy,
  and they both went to the LSU Medical School
in New Orleans, so it was no problem for them
  to swing through Baton Rouge on their way
to Massachusetts and give me a ride to the camp
  where we'd all been hired to work that summer,
even though they were the camp doctors and I was
  just a kid and a mere archery/riflery counselor at that.

Dickie was not only full of ideas and fun
  but was also one of those people who knows someone
in every town, so that whenever we got tired
  or hungry, we'd pull over, Dickie would get out
his address book, and within five minutes we'd be
  turning into the driveway of one of his friends,
such as a guy in Lynchburg, Virginia

named Stump who'd just finished a pizza and a six pack
  when Dickie called and who kept staring at Dickie
in disbelief and asking me and Art,
  "What did you say your name was?"

Then there was Dickie's friend in Arlington
  who had a beagle who sang along when Dickie
played the piano, and a third friend in Chevy Chase,
  Maryland who had played bagpipes for the Trinity College

Drum & Fife Corps and who said, "Watch this,
  the neighbors hate it" and went into his back yard
and lit into "McPherson's Lament" or something like that,
  and sure enough, all these old people came out
of their houses and said, "Now cut that out" and
  "That's it, I'm calling the cops"—pretty heady stuff
for a provincial sixteen-year-old, but nothing

compared to the prospect of meeting Mr. Try Me,
  Mr. I Can't Stand Myself (When You Touch Me),
Mr. Please, Please, Please, the unquestioned King
  of Rhythm and Blues. Of course, he wasn't there:
JB had gone ahead, probably by limo, but the Famous Flames
  were all inside the Howard Johnson's, waiting
for their food to come and looking extremely hip
  in their shiny suits and skinny ties. Dickie and Art

and I sat at the counter and placed our orders—I remember
  having a chicken salad on toast and a strawberry soda made
with peppermint ice cream—but while we were waiting
  for our food, a guy sitting a few stools down from us
began to pitch a fit. "This malted tastes terrible,"
  he said, only he pronounced it "mwalted,"
and he held up his malt glass and waved it

at the counter girl, who was about my age and
  extremely pretty, and said, "There's something wrwong heh,
something very wrwong," and he kept waving the glass
  at the counter girl and trying to get her to taste
the malt, and by now she was nearly in tears,
  and the guy was kicking up such a ruckus
that even the Famous Flames had stopped being cool
  and were looking our way. It was probably just

a soapy glass, if anything, but the guy was making
   such a fuss that finally Dickie got up and went over
to him and said, "Richard Biles, M. D."
   (which wasn't quite true, since he still had a year
of medical school left), "may I see that glass, please?
   Hmm, yes. Yes," said Dickie, sniffing the malt
suspiciously, "it's as I feared." Then he put one thumb

on the guy's eyelid and peered in. "Sir, you have
   been poisoned. Someone has put poison in your
malted milkshake. And there is no cure."
   The guy stared at Dickie for a second, eyes bulging
with terror, and went, "Gaaahh!" and ran out into
   the parking lot, clutching his neck with both hands.
The counter girl burst out laughing, and so did
   the Famous Flames, who gave each other

complicated handshakes and told Dickie
   he was all right and autographed a Howard Johnson's
place mat for me, and as we went out the door,
   I looked back, and the counter girl had put a little kiss
on her finger tips and she blew it at me, but I was so
   surprised that I didn't catch it and berated myself
later for having been so clumsy and stupid,

and off we went to Cape Namequoit in Orleans, Massachusetts,
   where Dickie and Art passed out aspirin and bandaids
and calamine lotion, and I taught kids
   not to shoot themselves and even to hit the target
from time to time, and the summer went by in a hazy blur,
   the best thing about it having already happened
at the very beginning. Now obviously
   I still think about those days a lot, but when I do,

I think less of Dickie Biles and the Famous Flames
   and the poisoned guy and the pretty counter girl
and more of Art Kennedy, who was one of those big,
   bearish men whose solid calm was a welcome contrast
to Dickie's excitability and my provincial self-doubt

and who never said much the whole trip but looked out
the window a lot and whom I now associate with the other,

more celebrated Kennedys: John and Bobby, who would be
    shot dead in a few years, and tragic, lucky Teddy,
who would drown poor Mary Jo Kopechne in a pond not far
    from the camp where we worked and then go scot free,
whereas anyone else would have done serious time.
    There was something in Art's gaze as he looked out
of Dickie's car window, and the shadows grew long,
    and the sun went down over Lynchburg and Arlington

and Chevy Chase. The summer sped by more quickly
    than anyone could have imagined, and with it came
the Cuban missile crisis and, soon, rumors
    about John and Marilyn, and then Oswald and
the grassy knoll and the Freedom Riders the summer
    after that, and then the war and hippies and acid
and the Summer of Love, and then rumors

about Bobby and Marilyn, and then Sirhan Sirhan
    and Malcolm X and the police riots in Chicago
and the three days of Woodstock and the bridge
    at Chappaquiddick, all of it springing from
that sad, gaudy amalgam of touch football and nookie
    and Harvard diplomas and boat races off Hyannisport
and conspiracies and mob connections
    and horsedrawn carriages going up Pennsylvania Avenue

to the sound of muffled drums. What I tell myself
    is that Art was the brother who got away,
who deliberately turned his back on that whole bright,
    shining family, its blood hot with poison even
in those innocent days, though no one could have known it
    at the time. He was the smart Kennedy, the one who didn't
say anything because he knew no one would believe him.

Lurch, Whose Story Doesn't End

It's as though you're snowed in at the airport forever.
   Or you're sent to purgatory, say:
you spend all this time learning the story of your own life
   and then you don't get to tell it.
This one begins with me and the other guys
   carrying stuff into our half of the house
we had rented for spring break,

   while Whit Little takes his clothes off on the beach,
folds them carefully, and walks into the waves.
   A few minutes later, the girls pull up in their car.
They have their swimsuits on under their blouses and shorts,
   so they took off their clothes, too,
and run down to the water as Whit smiles
   and greets them, his hands on his hips.

Whit, Whit! they scream. How's the water?
   Great, you'll love it, he replies.
Just then the tide goes out with a great sucking roar,
   and Whit is left in water up to his ankles,
his nuts tight from the chill
   and his big, floppy, half-hard penis
sticking out like an elephant's trunk.

   Sandra Broussard, who is in front, digs in her heels;
the other girls scream and crash into her and fall
   in a big heap on the sand. Then they run back up
the beach again, still screaming but laughing now,
   and put their girl stuff into their half of the house
we'd all rented together in Grayton Beach,
   half a day's drive from Baton Rouge.

That night there is a poker game in the kitchen.
   Maybe Lurch is one of the card players;
if that were the case, his story would begin here,
   but I can't remember where he first comes in.
The girls spin records and dance in the living room,

except for Kathy Smiley, who sits and watches the poker game,
not saying anything. Kathy doesn't look so great;

    she'd been on the beach all day in her two-piece,
refusing everyone's offer of lotion because,
    as she kept saying, she was going to get
the "basis" of a tan first and then
    start smearing on the Coppertone later.
She'd been light pink at supper
    and by now she is a deep red, bordering on purple.

Around one, most of the girls have gone to bed,
    and the guys are tired of the beer and the cards,
so we get up to go to our rooms, everybody but Kathy,
    who just sits there. Come on, Kathy, bedtime,
say the guys, See you tomorrow, come on, get up, get up.
    I can't, says Kathy, and everybody stops,
and the guys who have left the room come back.

    What? says someone. I can't get up, says Kathy,
I can't move, and she begins to cry.
    There is a quick discussion, and then the Wilkersons,
two pairs of brothers who are also cousins
    and who played football together in high school,
get on the four corners of Kathy Smiley's chair.
    One, two, three, says somebody,

and the four Wilkersons lift Kathy Smiley up,
    chair and all, and take her out
to Robby Wilkerson's truck, the bed of which
    had been filled that morning with cans of tomato soup
and boxes of evaporated milk and jars of peanut butter
    and loaves of white bread and case after case of beer
but which is now empty.

    And so we take Kathy Smiley
to the Okaloosa County Regional Medical Center,
    where she spends the next ten days
on painkillers. Kathy finally comes around,
    but it's long after we'd all driven back to Baton Rouge

and returned to our classes at LSU
    and our regular boy- and girlfriends.

And that could be the end of a story,
    though not the story of Lurch,
since he hasn't even appeared yet,
    except perhaps as one of the nameless guys,
the one who says What? to Kathy Smiley, for example,
    or who signals for the Wilkersons to pick her up.
Surely there's enough for a story already:

    there's Whit Little and his big semi-hard dick,
then the serious matter of Kathy Smiley's burns,
    and, finally, Kathy's eventual recovery.
Lots of stories work this way:
    with the joke (Whit), the big scare
(Kathy gets severely burned) and then
    the brow-wiping moment of relief (Kathy gets better).

It would be the story of a day
    in the life of some nice middle-class kids,
half of whose names I've long since forgotten.
    I don't think anyone married anyone else in the group,
although most of them did marry and have children,
    and a good many divorced and probably drank too much
on occasion and fudged on their taxes

    but otherwise had lives much like the day
we had all just passed together,
    lives with some ups but some downs, too,
some levity and some pain, yet nothing
    nobody couldn't get over.
The story so far is their story,
    and it's probably *the* story for most people.

But it wouldn't be Lurch's story if it ended here.
    Lurch hasn't even appeared yet, and it would've been better
if he hadn't appeared at all, if he'd been one
    of the ones whose names I can't remember.
In fact, Lurch got into and then out of the story

without me knowing it. I'd gone to the hospital
with Kathy Smiley and the Wilkersons;

    someone was needed in the truck bed
to hold the fourth leg of Kathy's chair
    so Robby Wilkerson could drive to the hospital.
Naturally we thought the story had gone with us,
    but when we got back to the house in Grayton Beach,
we found the story was still there
    and had been all along.

All the lights in the house were on;
    the house was so brightly lit
that it looked as though it were on fire.
    And everyone was walking around outside,
either crying or vomiting. One of the guys,
    Bob Fisher, had been drinking all day long
and had begun to lie down in front of cars

    as they bounced along the little beach road.
He'd pretend he was an accident victim,
    and when the drivers got out to see if they could help,
he'd cackle and lurch off into the bushes.
    In fact, we called him Lurch after the character
on *The Addams Family,* since he was big
    and ungainly and had a low voice.

As the Wilkersons and I took Kathy
    to the hospital, some of the other guys
decided to follow us, so they piled into
    Greg Cangelosi's jeep and took off.
Lurch, who was really drunk by now,
    ran down the road a little bit, hid in the bushes,
and flopped down in front of the jeep;

    in all the excitement, Greg didn't see him
and, in fact, didn't even know he'd run over him
    until one of the guys looked back
and saw Lurch lying there with his legs broken
    and his chest crushed.

And that's the scene we came back to
    after we'd taken Kathy to the hospital.

That's the problem with the story of Lurch,
    because it's the last thing I remember:
the unnatural light that streamed out of the house,
    and everybody outside, crying or vomiting.
Obviously the police were brought in,
    and Lurch's body was taken somewhere,
probably to the hospital where Kathy was lying,

    coming in and out of consciousness
and thinking during her wakeful moments
    that the story was still there with her.
And Lurch's parents must have been notified,
    and surely somebody led a prayer at the beach,
and there must have been a funeral
    when we got back to Baton Rouge again.

But all I remember is the chaos
    and the bright, hazy pain
that streamed from the windows
    of the house in Grayton Beach
and then nothing; the next thing I knew,
    I was sitting in class again,
trying to make sense of what my teachers were saying

    and wondering whether I should keep going out
with the girl I'd been dating.
    She was really pretty, but she was getting
more and more sarcastic all the time,
    so I was thinking of asking out a girl
I sat next to in The Eighteenth-Century Novel
    who was plainer but had a better disposition.

So, on the one hand, it was as though
    nothing had happened. On the other,
the worst thing that could have happened, did.
    I'm still not sure where the story of Lurch begins.
All I'm sure of is the bright, painful middle,

the house with that horrible light coming out of it,
and everybody out front, sobbing and throwing up.

And it's obvious that the story can't end there,
sans dénouement, as it were. But if I'm not sure
    where the story of Lurch begins,
maybe it doesn't have to have an ending.
    Or maybe some stories simply don't end.
Certainly the story of Lurch never ends;
    it just stops being told.

Listening to John Crowe Ransom Read His Poetry

I am waiting for my wife to get dressed
so we can drive over to campus for
    the regular Tuesday poetry reading which,
when you consider that it takes place, say,
    forty times a year, means that, along
with the readings sponsored by other groups,
    there are maybe sixty poetry readings annually
of all kinds—benefits, slam poetry contests,
    even anti-poetry readings—in our little town
of less than a hundred thousand people.
    So while everyone decries the dwindling audience
for poetry, I don't see it: when I was in college,
    we almost never had readings, and I didn't go
to any until I was a senior and John Crowe Ransom
    came to the LSU campus to read his poetry.

Ransom was pretty much it as far as
Southern poetry went—at worst, he was tied
    with Robert Penn Warren—what with him being
an Agrarian poet and then a member of
    the Fugitive group and, later, founder
of *The Kenyon Review* as well as author of
    Chills and Fever, Two Gentlemen in Bonds,
The World's Body, and all these other great collections.
    So everybody was pretty excited about his coming,
with the exception of my then-girlfriend,
    who was majoring in something called
Clothing and Textiles and whom I was dating
    because I thought it would be refreshing to go out
with somebody who had ideas and interests
    different from mine—big mistake—and who was

now beginning to pull away from me
and all the "impractical" things I adored.
    She said no, she didn't see what
the big deal was, but yeah, sure, she would
    go along to see the famous poet since

it meant so much to me. So I put on
    my best clothes and she puts on hers
and off we go to the auditorium,
    where everyone is waiting, all dressed up
as though they are at the prom.
    In those days, men still wore coats and ties
and women wore dresses to football games,
    so you can imagine how gussied up they are
for a poetry reading. We find good seats
    in the middle, and everybody else files in

    pretty quickly, until there are maybe
seven hundred fifty or eight hundred people there.
    And then Ransom comes out, dapper little
white-haired guy close to eighty years old,
    and starts reading these terrific poems:
"Blue Girls," "Piazza Piece," "Captain Carpenter,"
    and, to be sure, "Bells for John Whiteside's Daughter."
In his semi-ironic, semi-whimsical way,
    Ransom is just knocking everybody out,
even though he seems to weary as the evening goes on
    and spends more and more time shuffling his pages
between poems. My girlfriend and I are sitting
    behind one of my teachers, Dr. Fabian Gudas,
who is quite bald and has a big, sweet, goofy grin,
    and his wife, whose name is Almena Meeks.

    And behind us is this big moron
who is in a couple of classes of mine
    and who impresses me as little more
than a blowhard as well as something of
    a mystery, since he is openly contemptuous
of literature and especially poetry,
    which he clearly thinks of as a craft
practiced exclusively by leftists and sissies.
    It is during one of Mr. Ransom's silences
that the moron says loudly to his date,
    "See that bald-headed fruit? That's my English
professor," whereupon Dr. Gudas swivels around
    and scowls directly at me, who begins

to stammer things like, "I didn't say you were
    a bald-headed fruit, Dr. Gudas; I mean,

I don't think you're a fruit. . . ."
The people around me who realize what has happened
    begin to laugh, my then-girlfriend included,
while the others begin to shush us,
    because by that time John Crowe Ransom
has started up again with "Here Lies a Lady"
    or "Janet Waking" or any one of a number
of his (and I think the word comes from
    a Jane Austen novel, though I can't remember
which one) superexcellent poems. The evening
    ended badly, I'm sure, with much teeth-grinding
on my part and quite a few snippy exchanges
    with my then-girlfriend, who had decided
to compound my shame by not only cataloging
    but also painstakingly analyzing a number

of minor humiliations I had endured recently
in her presence but had, until that moment,
    successfully forgotten. The funny thing
is that I don't remember anything at all
    about the fight or fights that must have ensued
and the subsequent breakup, only that
    I must have broken up with my then-girlfriend
at some point because otherwise I would be
    married to her and not the woman in
the other room who is trying on different
    pairs of shoes and asking This pair?
This pair? even though I keep saying that
    the latest pair is absolutely the perfect
choice, no doubt about it. What I do remember
    from that evening is the trivial though,

now that I think about it,
rather amusing exchange involving me
    and Dr. Gudas and that moron,
which vignette could have been scripted
    by Feydeau or Goldoni or one of the other

great farceurs, as well as
      the less flashy but more deeply satisfying
image of the somewhat donnish Mr. Ransom
      and the philosophical-fanciful tone
of his wonderful poems,
      which I have decided lately
to characterize by the adjective "marmoreal,"
      which means marble-like, though
in a warm manner—like flesh, in other words,
      but with the immortality of statues.

Mr. Andrews

I'd been hired by Sears to install appliances,
    but since I was just a 20-year-old college kid
working for the summer,
    the supervisor assigned me to Mr. Andrews,
who was older, shorter, and angrier than I was.
    Mr. Andrews' uniform always looked freshly pressed
and somehow never got wrinkled
    during those long, humid Louisiana afternoons.
And his hair, which was as black as anthracite,
    always seemed carefully combed,
though I never saw him touch it.
    But my uniform tended to be baggy and wrinkled;
my hair flopped in my face, which was the style then;
    and I tended to chatter about myself,
the girls I dated, and the movies I'd seen,
    blah blah blah, while Mr. Andrews drove the truck out,
did his part on the installations, handled the paperwork,
    and drove us back, all in a smoldering silence.

He could also drink scalding hot coffee
    as though it were ice water:
we'd stop at the Toddle House
    and he would turn off the ignition
and jump out of the truck and slam the door
    while I was still asking if he thought it would rain
and if I should roll up my window;
    by the time I got inside,
he'd have already ordered two coffees,
    and when they came, he'd drink his in one big gulp,
whirl around on the stool,
    scatter some change on the counter,
and be outside while I was still blowing on mine
    and trying to get at least a couple of sips in me
before I had to put the cup down and run after him
    and hurl myself into the already-moving truck
as it crunched across the oyster shells
    in the Toddle House parking lot.

Because it was summer,
        we spent most of our time installing air conditioners,
and Mr. Andrews always made sure that I carried
        the end with the compressor in it,
which accounts for about two-thirds of a unit's weight,
        though I said this didn't bother me
because I figured the extra work was good exercise
        and would add muscle to my skinny frame,
a concept Mr. Andrews thought asinine,
        as he did most of my ideas.
Besides, what were a few extra pounds to me?
        We both knew I was working for Sears just that one summer
before I went back to college and the pretty girls I dated
        and my look-alike friends and my promising
and well-compensated if still somewhat indefinite future,
        which was the real reason why Mr. Andrews and I
could have never gotten along anyway,
        even if we'd had anything in common, which we didn't.

Once we delivered a riding mower to a customer
        who'd either been drinking or just awakened from a nap.
We ran the mower down the ramp and onto the customer's carport;
        Mr. Andrews removed all the packing material
and fooled with the choke and turned some switches
        and then he motioned for me to go ahead, try her out.
I'd never ridden a power mower before,
        but I could see that it had an on switch,
three gears, F, N, and R, and a brake pedal
        the size of a dictionary; how difficult could it be?
I started the mower up, threw it into F,
        and shot forward across the carport,
almost smashing into the wall
        before I decided to take it out of gear.
But I missed N and went all the way to R
        and shot backward, almost hitting Mr. Andrews
and the customer, who came to life suddenly
        and shouted, "Whoa, now!"

In my panic I forgot all about the big brake pedal
        and rammed it into F again and shot forward

and then into R and went back and forth
     maybe a dozen times in a noisy, gear-grinding frenzy
while the customer ran alongside shouting,
     "Whoa, now! Whoa, now!" and Mr. Andrews looked on
with his usual studied contempt until finally
     he reached over and turned off the ignition
and the mower coasted to a halt.
     Falling back on my college-boy glibness,
I said something about having given the machine
     a thorough check and now the customer
shouldn't have any problem with it,
     but I didn't fool anyone, least of all Mr. Andrews,
who finished the day without saying a word to me,
     although, since that's what he always did,
there really wasn't that much difference
     between this particular day and any other.

Besides the ACs and the occasional power mower,
     we had another job, one that had nothing to do
with installing appliances
     and that still seems strange to me
despite all the time that has passed since those days.
     It was to repossess wigs:
it seems that a lot of young women
     had put something down on a Sears wig
but then couldn't or wouldn't keep up the payments,
     so Mr. Andrews and I would be sent around
to retrieve the merchandise:
     we'd install a couple of air conditioners
in the morning before it got too hot,
     grab a quick coffee at the Toddle House
or maybe lunch at Vince's Bar and Grill,
     where, despite our differences,
we both had the same thing every day—
     two cheeseburgers "all the way" and two Barq's root beers—

drive out to wherever the delinquent wig owner lived,
     and pull the truck into the front yard,
whereupon Mr. Andrews would leap out, bound up
     to the door of the little ramshackle house or trailer,

go inside, and emerge what always seemed like
      a few seconds later with a wig box under his arm,
trailed by some miserable-looking single mother
      and a couple of unwashed kids.
I never heard what Mr. Andrews said
      to these resentful and disappointed women,
if he said anything at all,
      and just assumed they knew he was there for the wig,
so back it went into the box in silence
      and then out the door
with this little pissed-off-looking guy
      who jumped back in his stupid truck
where his doofus assistant sat with a big stupid grin
      on his stupid face as if to say, No hard feelings.

Mr. Andrews spoke to me exactly twice that summer,
      unless he said something during one of my frequent naps,
which I doubt. The first time was when we were installing an AC
      in a house that had maybe six young men living in it,
five of whom were acting nervous and polite
      the way people do when the guys from Sears are there.
But the sixth man, who was heavily tanned
      and wore nothing but a leopard-skin bikini
and thick eye makeup, kept sort of prancing around me
      and making dancers' gestures and groaning passionately,
while the other men alternately left the room
      to muffle their laughter and came back in
to see what new outrage their campy friend was up to.
      I just smiled and tried to heave the compressor end
of the AC into place while Mr. Andrews rode the whole thing out
      in his customary, that is to say, silent manner.
But when we got down the road a mile or so, he said,
      "I bet those old boys know how to lick a dick."

The only other time he said anything to me
      was when we were installing a washer-dryer combo
at the Kappa Kappa Gamma house on the LSU campus.
      The sorority girls were going to class,
and as they streamed past us
      with their teased and lacquered hair

and their flawless skin and their little trim figures
  and their happy, big-mouthed laughter,
Mr. Andrews watched them for a while and then said,
  "I wouldn't mind being stationed in these barracks,"
which was a bigger deal than I'm making it sound,
  not only because the summer was nearly over
and it was only the second thing he'd said to me the whole time
  but because he actually smiled as he said it.
When I turned in my uniform, the supervisor asked
  if I thought I'd be interested
in the Sears manager trainee program, and I said no,
  I didn't think I wanted to be anybody's boss.

The Afterlife

Shots and drafts? Ken would ask, and I'd say,
   Shots and drafts, and off we'd go
to some bar on Greenmount Street for jiggers
   of cheap whiskey and ten-ounce brews,
fresh from the tap, or just the beer itself:
   most days we had to get up early
and prepare for class or at least shuffle
   our note cards so that when our advisors asked,
How's the dissertation coming?
   we could say, Fine, I was just working on it,

and while a few beers never interfered with
   our scholarly activities, such as they were,
there is something about cheap whiskey
   that makes you want to throw furniture
through the window after a while—
   which we never did, although fighting
that impulse can be just as exhausting—
   so we'd usually save the shots for an occasion,
like the anniversary of the first edition
   of *Leaves of Grass* or Fats Domino's birthday,

and even our beer-drinking came to be
   rather systematic after a while:
Johns Hopkins U. was a real pressure cooker,
   and one way to deal with all the craziness
was to make a few rules for yourself
   and stick to them and then, when your own rules
were making you as crazy as the ones
   the professors were imposing, to go off the tracks
for a while but then get back on
   as soon as possible and with little damage done,

which is why we (a) always walked to the bar
   (b) never made eye contact with anybody
who was looking for an argument,
   and (c) drank as much as we wanted
as long as we got home by one.

Whereupon we would make cinnamon toast:
you're always hungry after you've been
    drinking on an empty stomach,
so I'd say, How about I heat up
    some soup or A sandwich would go good about now,

but Ken was insistent and usually got his way.
    He had a sweet tooth, and also I figured
maybe it was something everybody did in Detroit,
    where he was from and about which I didn't know
anything, being from Baton Rouge and thinking
    that anyone who came from a bigger city
was bound to know more about life than I did.
    Besides, Ken did all the work:
he'd turn on the oven and get out the butter
    and the cinnamon and the sugar

and prepare the bread slices and yank
    the broiler rack out and put the slices
on the rack and shove it back in,
    and while we were waiting,
we would talk about one of the Henrys,
    Adams or James, or our professors
or girls and how we wish we knew some,
    and we would brew tea, which was
Ken's other big passion after cinnamon toast,
    or have another beer if there was any.

And then we'd smell smoke,
    because we always burned the first batch
of toast; though far be it for fellows
    as chuckleheaded and unflappable as we were
by that point to become discouraged:
    Ken would shout, Get the window, Kirbs!
and I would raise the sash,
    and he would grab a fork
and yank out the broiler rack again,
    and there would be all this cremated bread—

a dozen slices, maybe, because Ken loved
    his toast, so we would make as much
as would fit on the rack, and I'd eat
    a couple of slices, and he'd have the rest,
but only after he'd pitched the first batch
    out the window: he'd get down
in a three-point stance and, with coordination
    uncommon to someone who had been drinking
all night, start forking those charred slices
    out the window, counting as he went:

One! Two! Three! And when the last one
    was gone, he'd put the fork down,
dust his hands off exaggeratedly,
    grin as if to say, That's that,
and start on batch number two,
    which always came out fine, because by that time
we were alert to the hazard of overdoing it,
    which we nonetheless did anyway, say,
twice a week for the year that we roomed together
    for a total of maybe a hundred times.

Now this was not that big a deal in our lives
    and certainly pales in comparison to
a lot of things I remember from grad school,
    but what I've always wondered is this:
our apartment was on the top floor
    of an eight-story building right by campus,
and people were always hustling past at every hour
    of the day or night, so if Ken
forked a dozen slices of burned cinnamon toast
    out the window every third day or so,

there must have been people passing by
    and being hit and saying to their friend,
You get hit by something?
    And the friend bends down and picks
up this flat square and turns it over
    and smells it and says,
Yeah, it's a piece of cinnamon toast.

And since most people are creatures of habit
and take the same streets at the same time,
     you have to imagine a couple of people

going by in March and talking about Nietzsche
     or the categorical imperative,
and suddenly all this toast comes flying down,
     and they look at the sky in disbelief
and then brush each other off and keep going,
     but a month later they're coming by again,
lost in a discussion of structuralism
     or the bicameral brain,
when suddenly another shower of toast falls,
     and they look at each other and say, Damn!

Or I can picture somebody saying to his friend,
     Come on, we're having a great time, let's go back
to my place and make coffee, and the friend says,
     Yeah, but don't go down Charles Street. . . .
Or say someone is having a crisis because,
     as Erik Erikson says, he half-realizes
he is fatally overcommitted to what he is not.
     Or, like Madame de Sévigné, a woman says
that what she sees tires her
     and what she does not see worries her,

and they're walking along,
     things have been up and down
in their lives lately, but they're down now,
     that's for sure, and they're thinking,
God, why bother, and then the first piece
     of toast hits them on the shoulder,
and another piece lands in the bushes
     a few feet away, and they look up,
and pow, a piece hits them right on the nose,
     but it's only cinnamon toast,

so it doesn't really hurt, and they pick it up,
     and this piece isn't burned so badly,
it's one of the ones that was in the front corner

of the broiler rack, and it's still warm,
and the person is a little hungry because
    he or she hasn't been eating so well lately,
so they figure, What the hell,
    and they take a little nibble,
and it's not so bad, and they walk home
    munching the warm cinnamon toast,

and when they get there,
    their husband or wife or lover says,
Jesus, where have you been,
    I was so worried, especially with
the state of mind you've been in lately,
    and the person gives a little smile—
not a big one, because it's not as though
    anything has really changed yet—
and says, Well, you know,
    the funniest thing just happened to me,

and they sit down and have a long talk
    and then get into bed together and keep talking
and they don't really make love but they do kind of
    nibble on each other and exchange big wet
open-mouthed kisses and finally fall asleep
    in each other's arms saying, Good night, I love you,
good night, I love you so much, good night,
    good night, and while this isn't the kind of scenario
that you see in a lot of literature—a few stories
    by Raymond Carver, say, or I. B. Singer—

nonetheless any number of contemporary paintings
    depict something very much like this kind of moment:
an astonished throng looking skyward, say,
    as a gigantic flock of wingéd toast blocks out
the stars and the moon. And this is just the type
    of thing you want to happen when nothing
is fun anymore and you know you have
    to make a change but you don't know how
and you can't help thinking,
    There's got to be more to life than this.

Electricity

Tonight Allen Ginsberg is reading
on the Johns Hopkins campus,
    and I think, Who better to ask
    about those references to electricity
    in Walt Whitman's poetry that seem
to go way beyond science
    and hint at what Whitman
    called the "adhesiveness"
of male comradeship as well as
    a more sexual "amativeness,"

a subject Whitman was
not always so forthright about,
    having been burned enough times,
    thanks to the frankness
    of some of his poems,
that often he wrote elliptically
    on matters he might have been
    more candid about
had he been less concerned
    with his image as America's poet.

But it is 1968 now,
and Ginsberg is America's poet,
    and therefore you can
    imagine my feelings
    when he begins the reading
with that poem of his that starts,
    "What thoughts I have of you tonight,
    Walt Whitman . . . ," the one
that goes on to mourn
    "the lost America of love."

And, sure, he does a lot of silly stuff,
like play that stupid harmonium
    as he brays those William Blake poems
    totally off-key, but he reads "Howl"
    and his other great poems, too,
and overall it's just

a terrific evening,
        and I'm sitting there lapping it up
and smiling and nodding
        and checking out my fellow poetry lovers,

        some of whom are wearing
really just the most amazing outfits
        of paisley and velvet
        and gauzy fabrics of all kinds
        and wrist bells and head bands,
and there's incense in the air, and pot,
        and everybody is sort of sexed up
        and happy, and me, too,
though at the same time
        I'm obsessed with this electricity crap.

        I mean, you can see why
Whitman was gaga over it:
        if you're a mystic, any period
        in history should be as good as any other,
        but to know that you can send
a charge down a wire the way
        you can pump water through a pipe
        and then go from there
to the telegraph, telephone,
        electric lights for houses—

        it's as though the laws of physics
are complying at last
        with the most ardent desires
        of the soul and also as though
        science and democracy and progress
are on our side, really,
        instead of being sinister forces
        designed to wreck the world
and put the worst people
        over the rest of us.

        So the second the reading is over,
I make a beeline for Mr. Ginsberg,
        only every hippie in Baltimore
        is hoping either he'll answer

        their questions or listen to
the answers they have for him,
        not that he has asked,
        and also my professors are going
to seize Mr. Ginsberg and bear him off
        to the post-reading party

        unless I make my move really fast,
so after he has told the umpteenth hippie
        that, yeah, sure, peace will come,
        only we've all got to work on it together
        and also be sure to chant and meditate a lot,
I see my chance and blurt out,
        "ExcusemeMr.Ginsbergbutwhatsthedeal
        withWhitmanandelectricitybecausethere
seemstobealotofitinhispoetrybut
        hereferstoitprettyunconventionally,"

        and Mr. Ginsberg just lights right up
and halts his shambling walk
        toward the faculty station wagon
        and turns and raises both hands
        and smiles and says, "Easy—
you know what amativeness is?"
        and I say sure, and he says,
        "Well, among gays at that time,
amativeness was electric, and one person
        could pass it along to another,

        and especially young gays
to older ones, so that an older gay
        could literally charge up
        his batteries if a young guy screwed him,"
        and I'm standing there like, Hmmmmm,
so he says, "I found this out
        from a lovely man named Gavin Arthur,
        an astrologer who lived in San Francisco
and the grandson of President Chester Arthur,
        and I slept with him, and he had slept

        with this English poet named Edward Carpenter,
and Carpenter had slept with Whitman,

so there's a line of transmission there,"
and I am just about to make a joke
        and say, Yeah, a power line,
but just then the two groups
        vying for Mr. Ginsberg's attention collide,
    with the hippies on one side crying,
Mr. Ginsberg, man! and the professors
        on the other going, Allen, over here!

    So I figure I'll go my way,
but not before diving back
        into the melee to shake his hand,
    which is a little
        like that scene in *Moby-Dick*
where Ishmael and his shipmates are up
        to their shoulders
    in a barrel of spermaceti
and they're squeezing the lumps
        out of it so it can be used

        to make cosmetics and candles and soap,
and Ishmael thinks,
        " . . . a strange sort of insanity
    came over me; and I found myself
        unwittingly squeezing
my co-laborers' hands in it,
        mistaking their hands
    for the gentle globules,"
and while I'm certain I did shake
        Mr. Ginsberg's hand,

        there's probably no way he'd know
or even care that he shook mine.
        So as far as the line of transmission goes,
    we skipped that part,
        but a handshake is a handshake,
and I really do think that
        if you ever shook my hand,
    at least I could give you
this little one-volt number:
        like, zzzzzt.

Neighbors

One day it's the shy couple
 with the quiet kids,
and the next it's Brandi and Marlys,
  farm girls from Mayo, nursing majors
  who either hold hands and twirl each other
  square-dance style in the parking lot
at three a. m. as they sing I'M THE LUUUCCKIEST
  GURRRL IN THE WHOOOLE U.S.A.!
  or else slug it out in broad daylight,
  rolling around on the lawn
and punching the way guys do,
  trying to loosen teeth and break noses
  as they scream bitchbitchbitchbitchbitch.

Once Marlys threw a McDonald's strawberry shake
  at Brandi and missed,
but that pink goo stayed there all summer;
  it got rubbery and then hard,
  and after a while tires didn't even make
  tread marks in it any more.
Those were dog days, when "the sea boiled,
  wine soured, and dogs grew mad,"
  as the old almanackers used to have it,
  but otherwise a great time for me.
First real job, new town, new neighbor:
  Joan, a colleague, moved into
  the long-vacant apartment overhead.

That fall I taught a seminar
  on one of the great tropes, the doppelgänger:
Edwin Drood, Dr. Jekyll, Dorian Gray,
  the Prufrock who prepares a face
  to meet the faces that he meets.
  And if Brandi and Marlys continued
to have their ups and downs,
  Joan knew how to get to a party plateau
  and stay there, as I saw it,
  because two or three times a week

she'd have these galas that weren't loud,
        exactly, but resolute—dogged, I'd say,
    in their pursuit of fun:

            I'd be reading a book or grading papers,
        and suddenly I'd realize the music was up,
    people were talking and laughing
        and flirting with each other,
            drinks were being spilled and cigarettes lit
        until either I went to bed
    or simply noticed that
        it was quiet again and glanced upward
            and thought no more than
        Hey, party's over, if that.
    Joan and I were on some kind
        of committee together,
            and one day the chair called to remind me

            of a meeting and to ask
        if I'd leave a note for Joan,
    because he'd called her all evening
        and apparently she wasn't in, and I said,
            I think she's having some people over
        because I can hear them up there,
    so I'll stick my head in,
        and as I went upstairs,
            the party noise got louder
        and then really blared
    as Joan answered the door in a black dress
        and costume jewelry and stocking feet,
            a highball glass in one hand

            and a big grin on her face.
        David! she said. Come in!
    And I said, Just wanted
        to remind you about that meeting, Joan.
            Meeting? She looked puzzled
        for a second and then said,
    Meeting! Certainly!
        Make yourself comfortable

while I get my little book,
and she disappeared into her study
as my mouth fell open
and I heard somebody say, Whaa?
because that apartment was completely empty,

and the party sounds were coming from
a big reel-to-reel tape recorder on one wall
that was spooling out the canned merriment
I'd been overhearing for months.
Just then Joan came back
with her appointment book:
Thank God you reminded me, she said,
now what'll you have to drink?
Oh, I'd better be getting back, I said.
Cheers, then. Maybe next time.
Yeah, next time, I said,
and she smiled and wiggled her drink at me
through the half-closed door.

The next morning,
I was still trying
to wrap my mind around that one
when I stepped out on
what was evidently the aftermath
of yet another brawl between the farm girls:
Brandi lay on her side crying,
her hands between her thighs,
as Marlys stood over her.
She flashed me a grin
and a bright Hi!
and then bent over the sobbing Brandi
and muttered, That'll learn you.

The Money Changer

When I arrived in Bogotá,
the first thing I wanted to do was change money,
  but Bill said not to use the banks
because he knew a black-market money changer
        who'd give me a much better rate.
So we went up to the eighth floor of this building
  and buzzed a door with an import-export logo on it.
A secretary looked at us quizzically
        and then went in the back to find her boss.
The front office was a dusty room with a bare desk in it
  and a cabinet that had a couple of curios on one shelf
to represent whatever it was that was supposed to be
        imported or exported. The boss came in all smiles
and handshakes and gave me one and a half times
  the official rate for my travelers cheques,
and he and I and Bill made a date to go out
        to dinner together the following week.

        Meanwhile, Bill and I were going camping
on the coast with some friends of his,
  so we bought provisions and packed our bags
and hired a driver to take us to Buenaventura,
        which was a sort of rough port town
from which we'd catch a boat to the campsite.
  There were six of us, three men and three women,
and we spent the night
        at a huge white colonial-style hotel
which prompted a lot of joking
  about how we expected Humphrey Bogart
to walk in at any minute
        and get us involved in some kind of dangerous
yet thrilling enterprise, like gun-running
  to the beleaguered rebels who either were
or were not in the vicinity, depending
        on which newspaper you read.

        The next morning Bill and I went down
to check on boat times and saw some enormous black guys

with shirt-splitting muscles jabbering away in Spanish
as they tossed around these fifty-gallon drums
        of molasses or cooking oil or cocaine extract as though
they were cans of soup. After a while,
  we felt sort of small and white,
so we went back to the hotel, where one of the women
        said that she had epilepsy
and had brought her Dilantin but forgot the syringe,
  and did we think it would be okay
if she just broke open an ampule and swallowed the stuff?
        Bill, who'd had medical training, gave her
a dirty look and went out to see what he could find
  in this little town that didn't have a pharmacy,
much less a doctor, though he finally did get a syringe,
        I think maybe from a veterinarian.

        The sea was really rough,
and when we got to the campsite,
  the crew put one end of this skinny plank
on the dock and then motioned for us to run down it;
        we had to wait for the boat to heel all the way over
in one direction and then jump on the plank
  and run onto the dock as quickly as possible
before the boat started heeling back the other way.
        Once we got the camp set up,
we all went down to the beach for a swim.
  The women took their tops off, but when they shouted
for the men to remove their suits, we wouldn't,
        because while we could see that the breasts of the women
looked all pretty and perky and pointy,
  once the cold Pacific waters struck our privates,
the result would be what's sometimes known as
        the old olive-in-a-bird-nest effect.

        Now all this was pretty exciting to me,
because although all I had ever wanted to do,
  ever since I was a boy and my mother urged me to
become a photographer for the *National Geographic,*
        was travel and have adventures and then come home
to some big cosmopolitan city like New York

while I waited for my next assignment.
But I'd lived in dinky places my whole life,
        and for the last ten years I'd been stuck
in the same little town; nothing had happened there
  except a divorce which was about as dramatic
and interesting as the marriage
        that preceded it. I mean, I had a job,
but that wasn't really going anywhere,
  and it was getting kind of difficult
for me to tell the difference
        between one year and the next.

        Within three days, all six of us had intestinal parasites,
and so we decided to go back. As we left Buenaventura,
  we were stopped by a platoon of soldiers
with automatic weapons who searched our van
        for forty-five minutes before letting us go.
We were so happy when we got back to Bogotá
  that we drank too much aguardiente
and had terrible hangovers the next day.
        The woman with epilepsy
said she'd been to my little town
  only once in her life, and that was late at night,
when she and a boyfriend had stopped at the Western Sizzlin'
        on Tennessee Street, where they were the only customers,
and as they ate their steaks, one of the bored waitresses
  looked at the boyfriend and said to her equally-bored
colleague, in a loud and uncaring voice,
        "Boy, I sure would like to fuck him."

        Then the third guy in the group
said that *he* had been to Tallahassee only once
  and was in his car looking for a friend who lived on one
of the little streets near the FAMU campus when he saw a man
        aiming a shotgun at something across the road;
the guy figured that when he pulled abreast of the man
  with the gun, he'd lower it and let the car pass,
but the man with the gun just stood there,
        like a patriotic statue, until the guy driving
slammed on his brakes; by now the shotgun

was sticking out across the hood of the car.
The man pulled the trigger; there was a bang and a flash
        and a loud "whark!" from the yard across the way,
and the guy in the car looked over in time
  to see this mutt flip through the air and fall lifeless
to the ground; evidently the man with the gun
        had just killed the bad dog of the neigborhood.

        The next night Bill and I and two of the women
went out with the money changer and his wife,
  and as we ate and drank rum and talked,
it gradually became apparent that the money changer
        had handled a lot of cash for some of the top people
in the narcotics business throughout South, Central,
  and North America, including a good many
who were connected with the CIA and other U. S. agencies,
        and as he talked, I felt the way I had
as Bill and I had watched the muscular black guys
  juggling those huge barrels back in Buenaventura.
The money changer seemed to be under a lot of stress;
        his manners were impeccable, but he talked loudly
and laughed just a little too much. On the other hand,
  I could see that he was really excited by his work
and got a lot of pleasure out of it,
        not to mention a great deal of nontaxable income.

        During a lull in the conversation,
the money changer turned to me
  and lowered his voice and said,
with the precise enunciation of someone who knows
        a second language fluently but doesn't use it every day,
"Tell me, David, exactly what is it that you do?"
  For a moment I thought I'd say something like,
You know how you look out an airplane window
        and you see that the wing has hundreds
of these little screws in it?
  Well, I'm the one who patented that screw design,
so these days I just more or less collect my royalties
        and jet from spa to spa. Either that
or I'd been drafted by the Celtics

but had blown out a knee in my third game
and had collected this huge settlement,
        so these days I just more or less. . . .

        By now, everyone at the table was looking at me,
so I said, "What was that again?"
  and he repeated his question, and I tapped my chest
and said, "You mean me?" and he said, "Yes, yes!
        What is it that you do?" So I took a breath
and tried to sound as though I didn't care
  and said, "Oh, I'm a university professor
in a small town in North Florida." The money changer
        dropped his knife and fork and pressed his hands
together on his chest; for a moment I thought
  he was having a heart attack, but then he said,
and I could tell from his tone that he was
        absolutely sincere about it, "To be a university
professor in a small town in North Florida—
  that must be paradise!" and I thought,
well, yeah, if you think about it,
        everybody's life is pretty interesting.

The Ghost of Henry James

"Enchantée!" says Mrs. Huntington, extending her hand,
        which I take, my jaw dropping onto my chest
and my brain going into gridlock
        as I tell myself, Think, Kirby, say something,
anything, but I'm just standing there like an idiot,

"there" being the courtyard of the Villa Mercede
        on the hill of Bellosguardo outside Florence,
a palazzo known as the Villa Castellani when Henry James
        not only lived in it but set part of
The Portrait of a Lady there, its heavily stuccoed

and cross-barred windows still suggesting,
        as it did when I first saw it two months earlier,
"the mask, not the face of the house,"
        a place easy to get into, thinks Isabel Archer
to herself, yet, once in, impossible to leave—

for me, impossible to enter, or so I thought that first time,
        so it was back down the hill to the city
and my students and class prep and lots of lovely meals
        and long, cold (but lovely) walks,
and then one night a woman comes by

(I don't have a phone) and introduces herself
        as Cherry Barney, who is a friend of a friend,
and promises to send her husband Steve to pick me up
        (I don't have a car, either) for dinner one night,
and when Steve comes, we make embarrassed small talk,

like, "Uh . . . where do you live?"
        the answer to which is, "Oh . . . up in
Bellosguardo," to which I say, "Do you know
        the Villa Mercede?" and Steve answers, "Oh,
I live there!" So that's where I dine that night,

in this big gloomy high-ceilinged place with
        paved tile floors and curious partitions here

and there that no doubt destroyed the shape of some
   marvelous rooms to make modern-day apartments,
but the best part is meeting this woman named

Mrs. Huntington, Steve and Cherry's landlady,
   who is 85 yet as lively as can be, confiding,
in French-accented English (she'd been born
   in Boston yet raised on the Continent) that
she "remeembaired playing at zuh feet of Monsieur

Henri Jame when he pay zuh veezeet," and I'm
   thinking, whoa, is this possible? It's 1973
at the moment, and a little quick subtraction
   suggests she was born in 1887,
so, yeah, maybe she had been around—

James began *The Portrait* in 1880 but returned
   to Florence in 1887, 1890 (when she would have been
three), and 1899 (twelve), so, sure,
   she could 'ave play at zuh feet of Monsieur Henri
when he pay zuh veezeet. The problem is

that I am doing this moron-level arithmetic
   when I should be asking Mrs. Huntington
about her impressions, to use one of James's
   favorite words, the little essences,
something he said, say. But hell, no:

I'm standing there holding her hand
   like she's a statue and going five from three
is eight, carry the one. . . .
   And by the time I get the dates right,
she has already make zuh retreat into zuh shadow.

So the next day it's dut-dut-dut-dut
   like a cartoon character to the library,
where I grab vol. I of HJ's letters and read
   "a large handsome apartment in town
in the same house as the Huntingtons"

(to HJ, Sr. on 26 Oct. 1869) and then
        "the Huntingtons, who were blooming
in their ruddy beauty" (to Elizabeth Boott,
        the real-life basis for Isabel Archer,
on 10 Dec. 1873), which familiar language

one uses only to describe friends
        of long standing, people one sees
again and again as one comes and goes
        and has lunch and tea and dinner
and plays badminton and croquet and watches

the children grow up and get married
        and have their own children who, decades later,
will remeembair play at zuh feet
        of cher Monsieur Henri
when he pay zuh goddamn veezeet!

So as soon as I can, I make a date to go back
        and take tea with Steve and Cherry,
and this time I have all the questions
        I was too dumbstruck to ask before,
like not what did he look like, which I knew already

from portraits, but how was his voice: high? Low?
        How low? Was he hesitant when he spoke or determined?
Did he like kids? Did he like you?
        But when I get to the Villa Mercede,
Mrs. Huntington is gone. "Gone?" I ask Steve.

"Gone," he says. "Gone where?" I say.
        "Don't know," he says. It seems that Steve
was walking back up the hill from town
        one afternoon and saw the portiere driving
Mrs. Huntington to the station; the car

had lots of bags on top, and when Steve
        asked the portiere where Mrs. Huntington
had gone, the portiere waved his hand vaguely
        towards the north and said "Aldilà,"

which Steve thought was a town for a couple of days

until he figured out that what the portiere
        had said was "al di là," which means
"beyond" or "outside," and that what the portiere
        was doing was being protective of Mrs. Huntington
and not blabbing her whereabouts to just anyone,

especially Steve, who was a foreigner.
        So there went my chance to question
the one person I was ever likely to meet
        who knew Henry James personally,
although at least I got to shake her hand.

And maybe she wouldn't have told me anything
        anyway. It's not as though she was knocked out
to make my acquaintance; she was nice on the surface
        but reserved, too, as James himself was said to be:
the kindest man in the world, really,

though if you started getting into his business,
        he would pull back into his shell
faster than a turtle; plus he wrote all those stories
        like "The Aspern Papers" which warn scholars
against snooping into writers' lives.

Still, I am pretty downcast,
        but Steve and Cherry give me several cups of tea
as well as a big slice of panettone,
        the Christmas cake with the currants in it,
and I am feeling a good deal better

as Steve and I take a stroll in the garden
        behind the villa and I turn and look up
just in time to see a man come out on the balcony
        of one of the apartments and scowl at us—
not "scowl," exactly, but "gaze down sardonically"

or something like that, this tallish man, dignified,
        portly in a way that says presence, not dissolution,

and peeved, perhaps, but mainly bemused,
     pursing his lips and knitting his brows
the way James does in the famous Sargent portrait,

and while he is obviously one of the other tenants,
     I say, "Who's that guy?" and Steve says—
and I have to hand it to him,
     it couldn't have been better if I'd planned it myself—
Steve says, "What guy?"

Something Wild

A production assistant is saying, "You gotta
get a doctor here right away. If ya don't,
I'll tell ya what's going to happen. What's gonna
    happen is, Jeff is going to stick a pin in that thing."
Jeff is Jeff Daniels (*Terms of Endearment, Purple Rose
of Cairo*) who is co-starring with Melanie Griffith
(*Body Double*) in a movie directed by Jonathan
    Demme (*Melvin and Howard, Swing Shift*) called

Something Wild, in which I have been hired
as an extra, and the "thing" is a large fever
blister in the very middle of Jeff's lower lip.
    I had been given only two instructions, to show up
    at seven a.m. and to dress upper-middle class,
so I have on my gray suit and a blue shirt
with a little beige check and a handwoven gray tie,
    although I am so eager to please that, with

the exception of my t-shirts and the pants I wear
when I mow the lawn, I have brought virtually
every other piece of clothing I own with me
    in the car in case I have to change.
But the head of costuming approves me
("You look nice. You look like a rich man")
and tells me I can get a cup of coffee.
    Ahead of me in line is Charles Napier (*Rambo*),

who says, "I didn't want to learn a bunch of lines,
but I told Jonathan I'd do it if he just wanted me
to beat the shit out of somebody."
    In this movie he plays a chef. Ahead of him
is Melanie Griffith, who is approached by
a large dog who wants her to throw a stick
for him. Since the dog has already wiped
    his muddy paws on my pants, I say, "Hey, Melanie,

watch out for the dog," but Melanie Griffith
knows better than to talk to wealthy strangers.

In the scene we are going to shoot today,
       Melanie and Jeff are finishing a meal in a restaurant
  when they find they don't have enough money to pay,
  so Melanie goes out and gets the car while Jeff
tries to talk his way past the restaurant owner
      but ends up literally running out on the check.

  One camera will catch Jeff barrelling out
  the door and diving into the car while another
will get the reaction shot: me; my film family,
      which consists of a wife and two teenagers;
  and the other diners looking up in surprise
  as Jeff runs off without paying.
But first something has to be done about
      that thing on Jeff's lip. He has been touching it

  all day, the way we do when we want to
  convince ourselves that something is just as awful
as it ever was. During rehearsal, Melanie has to
      kiss Jeff maybe thirty times. Melanie is a trouper.
  She still won't talk to me, though,
  so I am thinking of turning my attention to Jeff.
I look around for the muddy dog so I can say, "Hey, Jeff,
      watch out for the dog," but no luck.

  Meanwhile, the thing on Jeff's lip has become
  a small promontory, and when he rehearses the part
where he has to run out the front door,
      I notice he stops and puts his hands
  on his hips and stares at the ground hard,
  and at first I think he is motivating himself,
but then I realize he is probably trying
      not to pass out from the pain.

* * *

  Finally the doctor arrives, and while
  he is lancing the thing on Jeff's lip,
Jonathan Demme decides to rehearse the part
      in which Jeff argues with the restaurant owner,

who is played by Kenny Utt, who has produced
several Demme films and also had small parts in them.
What will happen is that Charles Napier, who plays
        the chef, who is also the son of the restaurant owner,

        hears the argument and comes out from behind
a curtain with a cleaver in his hand and says,
"Problem, Dad?" and Kenny Utt says, "Possible
        cash flow problem," which is when Jeff takes off
for the parking lot. But even though it is
a minor scene, Charles is a major actor,
so Jonathan looks around for a stand-in
        and picks me when he sees that I am about

        the right size and color. One lesson I learn
is that lighting is everything in the movies,
so for the next half hour or so I keep strolling out
        from behind the curtain and saying,
"Problem, Dad?" to Kenny Utt, who says,
"Possible cash flow problem." And then they stop
and the lighting director, whose name is Tak Fujimoto,
        runs a photometer over my face and adds

        and takes away screens and reflectors,
and we do the whole bit again. Problem, Dad?
Possible cash flow problem! Finally the light
        is perfect; Jonathan says, "First team!"
and the actors return. For the reaction shot,
the extras are herded into the dining room
and seated; some are given salad, some coffee,
        and some are actually brought plates of crumbs

        so that it looks as though different tables
are at the different stages of a real meal.
My "family" and I get plates of cannelloni
        and fettucini, and when they do extra takes,
they bring us fresh plates of actual food,
whereas other people keep getting fresh plates of crumbs.
Finally they get the shot right, and Jonathan
        actually says, "Cut! That's a take! Print it!"

* * *

He thanks everybody, and we head for our cars.
I pass Melanie carrying her son Alexander,
who has just wakened from his nap
      and is not happy. A production assistant
nips into a trailer and nips out again, pulling
the cellophane off a Gremlin doll, and Alexander
begins to yell with delight, which is
      when an idea comes to me. I used to have

the same dentist as the governor of Florida,
and once I had my year-old son with me
when I went for my semi-annual check-up,
      and the governor was sitting in the dentist's
waiting room, and when he saw William,
he said, "Looks like a smart baby," and
immediately I thought better of that governor.
      So there on the movie set, I say, "Hey, Melanie,"

and she gives me a drop-dead look, and I say,
"Looks like a smart baby," and she says, "Really?
You think so?" and comes over and we have a little chat.
      Anyway, *Something Wild* came out maybe six months
later, and it's pretty good, and you can
get it at your video store, and I'm actually
in it, though you have to look really hard,
      because they don't linger over reaction shots

the way they do over some other kinds.
And the score is also very good, so you might
want to buy that in addition to seeing the movie,
      which I really enjoyed making, though like
a lot of things I liked doing, it's a little
blurry to me since new experiences tend to
replace old ones. Not that it's possible
      to forget everything, because Jonathan Demme tends

to use a lot of the same actors each time
he makes a film, so you see them and enjoy them
on screen but you also think about the movies
           you've seen them in before, and your new
memories get mixed in with your old memories
and your perceptions of what's going on right now,
and the whole time you're getting more and more
           deeply involved with the story and you're sort of

channeling all the wild things in your own life
into this one narrative structure while,
at the same time, you're thinking
           of newer, wilder stuff that you wouldn't
have ever thought of before if you hadn't
gone to the movie, which you're also
looking forward to discussing with your friends,
           even while you're watching it.

                                        * * *

Right now it's late January and coming up
on the anniversary of the death of my father,
who died last year on February 8.
           A couple of days ago, I got a phone call
from a grad-school chum who told me that,
not our real father, but our *pater academicus*
had died: Charles R. Anderson, who directed
           my dissertation but mainly served as a model

of unfailing industry and cheer,
working hard right up to the very last.
So this is a sort of complicated time for me
           emotionally, and I try to stay busy and cheerful
myself, working hard and spending my leisure time
wisely instead of just lying around reading trash
or watching network television. Yesterday,
           for example, I went to see *Philadelphia,* Demme's

new movie. Let's see, there's Tom Hanks (*Punchline,*
A League of Their Own) and Denzel Washington (*Mo'*

Better Blues, Malcolm X) and . . . Charlie Napier
      as the judge! And . . . Kenny Utt as a juror!
  This morning, though, I open *The New York Times,*
and in the obits it says, "Kenneth Utt, 72,
Producer of Films Who Also Acted," and I can't
      believe either that he's dead or that I feel

     so bad about it, because when I catch myself
thinking, Jesus, I was just talking to him
yesterday, I remind myself, No, I saw him
      yesterday, but that was in a movie, and
  the other movie, the one he and I were in together,
is nearly eight years old now. I have a friend at work
to whom I had mentioned the phone call about Charles
      and who keeps up with the movies and who knew that

    I had been in *Something Wild,* and he too had seen
Kenny's obit, and I talked to him about all this and said
I feel a little silly because I don't understand
      why I feel as bad as I do about the death
  of someone I barely knew, and he said,
David, you keep losing your fathers,
and I said, I know, I'm about out.
      Then we didn't say anything for a while,

    and he wandered back to his office, and
then he came back and stuck his head in the door
and said, Thank God for the movies,
      and I said, I certainly agree with that,
  and he said, Anything playing now?
and I said, Well, there's always something,
and he looked at his watch—by then, it was
      rather late in the day—and said, Come on, let's go.

A Really Good Story

Alex Weiss, the guy who books bands, walks into the café
         where I am eating with my son Ian and says, David,
and I say, Alex, and Ian says, Who's that,
         and I say, that's Alex Weiss, the guy who books bands,
but what I don't say is that Alex is a hero of mine,

because one day I had stopped at the corner of Monroe
         and Call behind a carload of morons in baseball caps,
and Alex starts to walk across the street in front
         of them and when he gets even with the front bumper
of their car, the head moron hits the horn

just to make Alex jump, which he does, though
         to my amazement he sort of twists in mid-air
like a ninja and lands facing the morons
         and shots them one of the most excellent cobs
I have ever seen, a cob being what we called a bird

in Baton Rouge, Louisiana when I was a boy
         and a term my son Ian and I use in our private language
and which refers to, not the slipshod limp-finger
         arrangements you often see these days,
but the classical configuration of steely middle digit

and the two on either side tightly curled
         in rock-hard scrotal perfection, a menacing,
trifle-with-me-my-friend-and-you'll-get-this-
         up-the-poop-chute ideogram of eye-popping rage,
and that's exactly the kind of cob Alex Weiss is pitching

these morons, only it's even better than that,
         because while he is doing his mid-air ninja twist,
he's waving his arms around like a bodybuilder
         getting ready to strike a pose and when he lands,
his extended arm is pointing the way God's does

when he's jump-starting Adam on the ceiling
         of the Sistine Chapel, only Alex Weiss's arm ends

in this excellent cob he's made, and his whole body
        is quivering slightly with the tension of the pose,
as in Got it, nailed it, bite this, you dirtbags,

and the morons are clawing their cheeks with rage,
        they can't believe a skinny guy like that
is cobbing them off right in the middle of Monroe Street,
        and their car is rocking up and down as they fight
each other for the door handles so they can get out

and murder Alex Weiss, the guy who books bands,
        but just then the light changes and I see my chance
to get in on the tail end of the fun, so I hit my horn
        and lean out the window and say Hey, get that shitcan
out of the road, and the morons scream and beat their hands

against their heads in impotent fury, and the driver
        flips a . . . bird at me as Alex Weiss steps off as though
nothing's happened and goes his way, probably to meet
        some band he's booked. Now maybe two years later
I see Alex and this girl in line in front of me

at the East End Deli, and I say, Alex, and he says, David,
        and I say, You know, Alex, you're a hero of mine,
and he says, Hmmm?, and I tell this story, and the girl
        is going, Alexxx! partly in reproof but partly proudly,
and Alex is saying, I don't remember this,

and the girl is going, Alexxxxx! and Alex is saying,
        I don't remember any of this at all,
but it happened, guaranteed—I'm not saying I don't lie,
        but I don't lie in these poems. The only thing is,
do I want to tell Ian this story, because at 16

he has already got his man's body and is starting
        to get ideas about what a man does and what it means
to be a man and all that bio-philosophical horseshit
        boys have to go through before they realize
that none of it makes any difference anyway,

and I certainly don't want to suggest that
            he ought to go around answering every provocation
every baboon offers him, because, in circumstances
            that would have to be only very slightly different,
those morons might well have boiled out of that car

and grabbed Alex Weiss and yanked him to pieces
            and scattered his parts all over downtown Tallahassee.
On the other hand, it's a really good story,
            and Ian's head seems to be screwed on the right way,
so I go ahead and tell him, and, predictably,

he almost chokes on his andouille and crawfish pizza,
            saying, Really, Dad, really, auk-hargh-hrssh-hargle,
and just then our protagonist comes back through
            the café where we are eating and says,
David, and I say, Alex, and off he goes down the street,

and I go back to my veggie muffaletta thinking
            how nice it is from an aesthetic standpoint
for Alex Weiss to be, not some linebacker,
            but the guy who books bands and is skinny to boot,
because what would be the point if he too

had been a big dumb-ass? And just then I remember
            that when Ian was four or five, I used to read him
fairy tales, and the one he always wanted to hear
            was the story of Thumbling, the child of a poor peasant
who says to his wife, How sad it is

that we have no children! With us all is so quiet,
            and in other houses it is noisy and lively,
and his wife sighs and says, Yes, even if we had
            only one, and it were only as big as a thumb,
I should be quite satisfied, and we would still

love it with all our hearts. When the little guy
            comes along, he has all sorts of adventures
and even makes a lot of money for his parents
            because he is "a wise and nimble creature,

and everything he did turned out well," and not only

did this become Ian's favorite story, but when
        I got to his favorite line, he'd say, Read that again,
and I'd say, he was a wise and nimble creature,
        and everything he did turned out well, and Ian
would suck his thumb and smile and look off dreamily,

and I could tell he was thinking of the many benefits
        of being wise and nimble when he grew up
and all the fun he'd have and the rewards.
        That's a good story, too, isn't it?
David and Goliath, the tailor who killed seven

with one blow . . . they're all good stories.
        Nothing like a good story.
Once a coach said, Is your boy smart?
        and I said I think so, and the coach said,
Good, then he won't have to be tough,

which is not true, because, after all, an aphorism
        doesn't have to be right, just sound right.
I'd say be smart first and then only as tough as need be—
        you know, we really need every good story
we can lay our hands on.

Laughing

My wife's girlfriend Diane is visiting from California
and so, to make an impression, I have prepared
           an excellent meal of crawfish-stuffed eggplant,
rice pilaf, salad of mixed greens with Dijon dressing,
           and sorbet, and the two women have gone into the den
to finish the second bottle of chardonnay

           while I sit at the table and finish grading papers
for class tomorrow, and I am almost done when,
           through the thin wall that separates the two rooms,
I hear Diane ask, What's it like being married to Dave?
           Barbara says something I cannot hear, and then
there is a chuckle, two, a torrent of helpless laughter.

           My wife and her friend are laughing so hard in the den
that it reminds me of the time Will, age eight,
           asked me what an enema was, and I said, Well, you
fill this rubber bag with water, see, and then you take this hose,
           and you stick it up your butt . . . and that was it
for Will; he lay on his side and held his stomach

           with both hands, and his little matchstick legs churned
as though monsters were trying to catch hold of them,
           and he screamed so loudly I thought I was going to have
to take him to the doctor, but then he calmed down,
           though for two or three days after he would suddenly say,
Enema! and fall down and start screaming again.

           Meanwhile this other, this woman-laughter, is loud also,
though I certainly didn't mind the two friends
           having a good shout together, because that is one
of the things that Barbara and I do best, and
           team laughing got us over a good number of rough patches
in the early days of our marriage when there wasn't

           much money and the whole stepmother-stepchild issue
to boot. That was when we lived on Chestwood Avenue
           next to this guy named Azel Pruitt, whom Barbara

called Hazel Motes after the character in *Wise Blood,*
     so that sometimes I'd slip and say,
"Morning, Mr. Motes—I mean, Mr. Pruitt!"

     He thought I was an idiot already because
I wasn't always trying to fix stuff the way he did,
     like his central air unit, which he put a new motor
in one day, although, when he flipped the switch,
     the unit went whang! and shot up sparks
because he'd put the motor in backwards,

     so Mr. Motes not only burned up his central air unit
but also had to call the Sears guy anyway.
     The Moteses' house was about four inches from ours,
and one summer night when we had the windows open,
     Barbara and I were making out
on the couch in the den when suddenly

     Mr. Motes ran out into his yard to throw up.
You all right, honey? his wife asked,
     and Mr. Motes said, Yeah, I—EEERRRRCH!
He stayed out there about twenty minutes,
     fetching up his chop suey, and every time
we thought he was finished, up it would come again,

     and Barbara and I were laughing so hard
that we had to use our asthma inhalers,
     but you're supposed to hold the albuterol mist
in your lungs for as long as you can,
     so here we are holding our breaths
and BLOOORRRRCH! Mr. Motes cuts loose again.

     Now whether or not the two women are laughing at me,
surely I am by myself in a room that has
     less laughter in it with each passing moment.
Then again, some of the greatest laughter
     has been evident more by its absence than otherwise,
as when my colleague Reed Merrill and I

were giving papers at a conference in Sydney,
and the Aussies were a little huffy
            since they thought we were even more provincial
than they were, so Reed tried to placate
            them by describing his paper as pearls before swine,
and naturally the audience really bristled at that,

            but this didn't stop Reed, who launched into his paper,
and after he had finished, I said,
            Well, that was a great paper, but why did you
say it was pearls before swine, and he said,
            I didn't, I made a funny joke and said
swine before pearls, and I said, No, you didn't,

            you said pearls before swine, and he said,
Oh, shit, and put his head in his hands,
            and everybody had long since filed out
of the lecture hall, so the two of us
            were standing there in this huge empty space,
and the whole place was filled with silent laughter.

            Oh, well, at least the interior
and the exterior reality came together
            for a minute there, as it had done earlier
for Barbara and me, though not for Mr. Motes,
            who couldn't hear us anyway. So much for
the unifying property of laughter, which also divides,

            as it is doing tonight and also in the eighth grade
when we were studying France, and Meg Holmes was giving
            a report about Versailles, and she was explaining
that the Emperor liked his good times,
            so when he wasn't waging war on the rest of Europe,
"Napoleon had these big balls. . . ."

            From the den of my house, there is more laughter.
Then someone turns on the radio; I hear an old song,
            one of the shameless ones that says it's okay
to have no pride, it's okay to love someone

no matter how badly they treat you, and then
I hear the voices of the two women begging me

    to come in and dance with them. We do the Hitchhike,
the Swim. The song stops and another starts;
        Diane goes for more wine as Barbara slips into my arms
and we dip, glide, tango. I hear Diane in the kitchen now.
        She is laughing to herself as Barbara and I kiss,
long and slow, and keep dancing.

Sacred Monsters

The place to look for them
　　　　is London: the city is large,
but the part they hang out in
　　is small, and besides, the English
　　　　don't pester them the way we do,
so that, on a given day, you can, as I did,
　　see Samantha Eggar in Peter Jones,
　　　　Donald Sutherland in Harrod's, and
John Houseman in Simpson's-on-the-Strand,

　each confident
　　　　in the knowledge that no one
will try to grab a coat button
　　for a souvenir or scream
　　　　that they should die of cancer because
they won't slow down for an autograph.
　　The next day I see Liam Neeson
　　　　on location and Mary Elizabeth
Mastrantonio in a lamp shop,

and another time Albert Finney sits behind me
　　　　and watches Ian McKellen in *Macbeth*
just before tackling the role himself.
"Albert Finney!" I blurt, in defiance
　　　　of local custom, and ask
if I can shake his hand, and he says,
　　"Certainly," and when I ask him
　　　　why he is watching Ian McKellen,
he says he is doing his "homework."

That was the exception, though,
　　　　because most celebrities
are pretty hard to get along with,
　　at least over here.
　　　　Once Joan Baez gives me a look
that would have made a headsman weep.
　　This is in the L.A. airport;
　　　　I am slouching in a chair,
deep in my own thoughts, when Joan walks by,

and at first she gives me
        a casual glance but then
she does a hard double take,
    a real soul-piercer meant to determine
        whether I am a bad oscar
or just Joe Neckbone waiting
    to catch a plane. Evidently she decides
        on the former—I look in the mirror,
I see Joe Neckbone, but Joan's eyes say,

"Lift a finger, jackass,
        and you'll be looking
at a bloody stump."
    Since then, I've seen other celebs
        use this little number on fools
more audacious than myself;
    evidently the Joan Baez Total
        Meltdown Laser-Look is a necessary component
of every celebrity arsenal.

                        * * *

Things are a little different
        the night Mick Jagger
thinks I am going to kill him.
    This is in Mobile in 1972;
        I am maybe six rows from the stage
and have pulled out
    my little pocket telescope
        for an even closer look.
Mick crouches down really fast;

JFK and Bobby and Martin have been shot
        in recent years (which is something else
we do to our celebrities over here),
    and Mick must figure he's next,
        so I put the 'scope away ASAP
and hold up my empty hands
    so he can see I'm not packing.
        It's not as though
I am trying to scare him to death;

it's just that relations
        between celebrities and the rest of us
are always going to be edgy—not that
   it matters tonight, because, being a professional,
        ol' Jag turns an act of cowardice
into part of the show; he spins up from his crouch,
   karate-kicks at an utterly bored Bill Wyman,
        and catches a groove:
   "Brown sugahh, how come you dance so goood!"

I also see a lot of celebrities
        around the nightclub that's two blocks
from where I live,
   because even when I'm not there
        to hear the acts, I like to ride my bike
through the parking lot
   and listen to the sound check
        and watch the stars
   as they get on and off the tour bus,

and this one time I am talking to the guy
        who drives the equipment truck
for Hall and Oates, and I ask him
   who in the business is really nice.
        Stevie Wonder, he says:
whenever Stevie does a show,
   he goes to the hall early and sets up
        and then he has a barbecue out back,
   and anybody walking by can go to the barbecue.

So who's really nasty,
        I ask. Frankie Valli and the Four Seasons,
says the truck driver without hesitating,
   and then he pauses.
        Well, not the Four Seasons.
But Frankie Valli, whew!
   And the truck driver shakes his head
        like a man trying to get the taste
   of a bad lunch out of his mouth.

                    * * *

Then he has to move his truck,
        so I don't get the specifics,
but I imagine that Frankie Valli
  does the same kind of things
        Sinatra does, but then
you forgive Sinatra,
    because he's given us "All the Way"
        and "One For My Baby"
    instead of "Big Girls Don't Cry."

But the point is that
        you never know when your average bigshot
will lose his or her mind in public
    and throw haymakers
        at these slow-to-react paparazzi,
so that what you the consumer
    get is a blurry tabloid picture
        of, not your favorite recording artist
    or skinny, big-bosomed movie star,

but somebody who is suddenly
        all fist or shoe sole,
a person ordinarily given
    to pronouncements about personal integrity
        and artistic vision
yet who now seems to be measuring his performance
    against that of, not Enrico Caruso
        or Katherine Hepburn, but the great Kid Gavilan,
    i.e., he of the fabled bolo punch,

so that a reclusive but otherwise likeable person
        goes out in public for about five minutes,
and the next thing you know,
    he's bouncing around like a bat who's lost his sonar,
        as hysterical as the rest of us get
just before we cringe and say,
    "Aw, come on, sweet thing,
        that was the whiskey talking"
    or "Mike, I swear, he's just a friend."

But perhaps we deserve to have our *monstres*
       sacrés pound the living crap out of us,
because surely the best ones
  spend every spare second perfecting their art.
       It's a little like the paradox
of the absent-minded professor; do you want
  Einstein to discover the theory of relativity
       or do you want him to remember
where he parked his car that morning?

So it's best to think of, say, Emily Dickinson
       as, not an old crazy recluse, but someone
who resisted the conventional lures of wife-
  and motherhood (which, in the nineteenth century,
       meant multiple births and the risk
of early death from puerperal fever
  and sheer exhaustion) in order to make time
       for herself to write seventeen hundred
and seventy-five fabulous goddamn poems.

                  * * *

A few years ago director Jonathan Demme
       shot part of his film *Something Wild,*
starring Jeff Daniels and Melanie Griffith,
  in Tallahassee, and I was hired as an extra,
       which mainly entails lots of waiting:
we shoot from seven a.m. to seven p.m.,
  redoing our scenes over and over
       but for the most part standing around
while Jonathan changes the lighting

or suggests new dialogue or moves the actors
       until he gets just the right look,
and during the breaks, I keep trying to talk
  to Melanie, which I thought would be okay,
       seeing as how we are both film-industry
professionals, but she won't have it.
  Not that she is actually rude, but if,
       for example, I say, "First time
in Tallahassee, Ms. Griffith?"

she says, "Um-hm"
        and looks off into the distance.
Finally, though, Jonathan
    yells, "Cut! That's a take!
        Print it!" He thanks everybody,
and we head for our cars.
    I pass Melanie carrying her son Alexander,
        who has just wakened from his nap
    and is not happy.

A production assistant nips out
        of a trailer, pulling the cellophane
off a Gremlin doll; Alexander begins
    to yell with delight, and an idea comes to me:
        I used to have the same dentist
as the governor of Florida, and once
    I had my year-old son with me when I went
        for my semi-annual check-up, and the governor
was sitting in the dentist's waiting room,

and when he saw Will, he said,
        "Looks like a smart baby,"
and immediately I thought better
    of that governor.
        So there on the set,
I say, "Hey, Melanie,"
    and she gives me a drop-dead look,
        and I say, "Looks like a smart baby,"
    and she says, "Really? You think so?"

and we have a little chat about how to get
        a child to sleep through the night (you can't)
and how to find good day care (ask around),
    and as we're talking,
        I notice she has the sweetest
little feet—like, elves could hollow out
    a pair of jelly beans, and she could wear them
        for shoes—and then she says,
"Well, gotta go," and that's that.

                        *   *   *

Anyway, *Something Wild* came out
      maybe six months later,
and I'm actually in it,
  though you have to look really hard
      to find me. I enjoyed making the movie,
though like a lot of things
  I've enjoyed doing, it's a little blurry
      to me now, since new experiences
tend to replace old ones.

Not that it's possible
      to forget everything,
because Jonathan Demme
  tends to use a lot of the same actors
      each time he makes a film,
so you see them and enjoy them
  on screen but also think about the movies
      you've seen them in before,
and your new memories get mixed in

with your old memories
      while, at the same time,
you're thinking of new stuff
  that you wouldn't have thought of
      at all if you hadn't gone
to the movie,
  which you're also looking forward
      to discussing with your friends,
even while you're watching it.

And maybe the point about celebrities
      is that in their public, ritualized forms
they help us to organize
  and at least partly comprehend
      our own scattered experiences,
whereas when they're working
  or just hanging out
      they are just as miserable
and awkward as the rest of us.

I wish I'd known how to talk
        to celebrities when I met Joyce Carol Oates;
I was introduced to her at a party
    as someone who had reviewed a book of her essays
        and she said, "I think you must be
a fellow Canadian," and I said, "Sorry, not me,"
    and Ms. Oates gave me the this funny look
        and walked away, and the person I was with said,
"What was that all about?" and I said,

"She said I was a Canadian," and he said,
        "She didn't say Canadian; she said Conradian."
There had been an essay on Conrad
    in that book, and I thought, Well, crap—
        what a fool not to talk to Ms. Oates about
children, because even if she didn't have kids
    of her own, surely she has some adorable nephew
        who can't pronounce his r's and for whom
she'd throw herself under a truck.

                                        * * *

This other time I am waiting
        to catch a plane
in Tallahassee and I see
    a little guy in a brown suit,
        porkpie hat, droopy eyes—
the whole Saul Bellow Hallowe'en costume.
    "That guy thinks he's Saul Bellow,"
        I say to Barbara.
    "That guy is Saul Bellow," she replies;

later, we hear that he had a brother
        who owned an antique furniture business
in Georgia and who has just died,
    so probably Mr. Bellow has come down
        to clean up his brother's affairs
and get rid of the armoires and end tables.
    We board the flight to Atlanta
        and sit in front, while Mr. Bellow
takes an aisle seat toward the rear.

Now this is the author of *Seize the Day*
        and *Herzog* and *Henderson the Rain King*,
books among the first serious novels I'd read.
   So I keep turning around to look at him,
        but all the while I'm thinking,
Maybe I shouldn't have introduced myself
   to Albert Finney like that, because
        I might have disturbed him when he was trying
to analyze some quirk of Ian McKellen's.

But it's easy to convince yourself
        that you have something to say
to a celebrity,
   some vital bit of encouragement
        that will get them through a crisis,
because, with all that alienation,
   surely they have it worse than the rest of us.
        Thank you! they'll cry when they hear
what we have to say, Oh, thank you!

And they'll tell
        the other celebrities how darling we are.
So I'm looking back there
   and I'm thinking,
        Well, yeah, maybe I will say something,
though I wonder
   if he'll give me the Joan Baez treatment,
        but I figure, What the hell,
Saul Bellow's not some temperamental folkie.

On the other hand, he is a little old,
        and I sure don't want to give him
the Mick Jagger treatment!
   So as I pass his seat on my way
        to the bathroom, I pause for a second
so he can see I don't mean any harm,
   and then I say, "Hey, Mr. Bellow,
        you keep writing 'em, I'll keep reading 'em,"
and he gives me this look like, You jerk.

Crying

My wife says she has made up her mind
                    to cry really hard when her mother dies,
        and I say, How can you tell how sad
                    you're going to be,
because sometimes death comes
                    as a release (Henry James
        described his family as "almost happy"
                    following his mother's death),
and she says, I can just tell, and besides,
                    you don't know anything about crying,
        you never cry at the movies,
                    and I say, I do, too,
I just don't make a big deal out of it
                    the way you do,

and when Roy Orbison died,
                    you'll recall that I cried piteously,
        and not just because of the song, either.
                    I cried harder over Roy Orbison's death
than I have over the death of aunts, say,
                    though my wife is right about me
        not wanting to cry in public,
                    because I'm not one of those
tragically-handsome weepers
                    you want to wrap your arms around
        and to whom you say,
                    There, there, it'll be better soon,
you're so pretty when you're sad,
                    come on, give us a little kiss. . . .

My face gets all twisted and ugly
                    when I cry, like I'm really unhappy
        but also I have to go to the bathroom.
                    Yet I have learned
the one great lesson about crying
                    that women seem to have mastered
        better than men, which is that

a good old-fashioned bawl
will make you feel better instantly,
and so from time to time
I sit down and have a nice heartfelt sob,
but only when there's no one around
and no mirror so I can't see
what a gargoyle I've become.

Too, I honor the great statesmen
of crying, the octogenarian James
Cagney who said crying comes easily
at his age as well as the defeated
presidential candidate Adlai Stevenson
who said that it hurt too much
to laugh but that he was too big to cry,
a surefire indicator that he had anyway.
Animals can't cry, and therefore I feel
sorry for them, but not so sorry
that I'm going to cry over it.
I'll probably cry when my own mother dies,
and certainly I've cried
at her condition right now:

she's ninety-two and hard of hearing
and nearly blind and so weak
she has to use a walker,
but those things don't make me cry.
What makes me cry is her pluck
and high-spiritedness in the face
of all this adversity;
why, just the other day she fell down,
and, as she lay there on the floor,
the paramedics were cackling like geese
at her retorts, jibes, and one-liners,
and you'd have to be brain-dead
not to laugh and cry simultaneously
at the indomitable spirit of such an old lady.

I know I'll be saying goodbye
to her soon, and when I think of that,

I think of the morning
            I was listening to NPR
and an Irish songwriter was talking
            about his mother,
    who had Alzheimer's,
            and it got to where the family
couldn't care for her anymore,
            so finally they had to put her in a home,
    and as he sat there holding her hand
            with her all scared and him, too,
he felt his big heart breaking
            because there was nothing he could say to her

and nothing he could do
            to keep her out of this hell
    she was climbing down into,
            and then he remembered
what she used to say to him
            when he was a little boy
    and she'd take him to school,
            and he didn't want to go, and he'd cry,
and she'd squeeze his hand and say,
            "Goodbye, love, there's no one leaving,"
    and that's what he said to his mother
            as they waited for the attendants to come,
Goodbye, love, there's no one leaving,
            goodbye, love, goodbye, goodbye.

Sad, isn't it? Of course
            we all know that when we cry
    for our agéd parents,
            we're really crying for ourselves,
yet who deserves our tears more?
            Ever since I was born, it's been the affair
    of the century: myself and I!
            Never have two lovers been more tender
toward each other, more beautiful
            in each other's eyes, even if
    our waists are thicker now, our hair gray.
            Look, everyone is crying;

they can't bear to see us go!
            And see how ugly they are!

Ha, ha! That's the real tragedy!
            Why, they're even more hideous
      than we are when we cry!
            They're crying so hard they're falling down,
and for a moment we are happy
            they can afford us such excellent amusement,
      but suddenly a suspicious thought
            crosses our minds—
what if they are crying for themselves
            as we have cried for ourselves
      when we seemed to be crying for others?
            But no, no, it must be us
they are crying for, for this time
            surely the gods themselves are dying.

Sex Therapy

Miranda (not her real name) and I
are having dinner with another couple
and really enjoying ourselves
when suddenly the husband
puts his arm around his wife's shoulders
and gives her a little squeeze,
and she says, That's three, Wally!
and Miranda says, You count hugs?
and the woman says, The therapist
says Wally has to hug me
three times a day, and on my side,
I get to talk about sex
whenever I want to,

and I can feel my face burning,
and I look over at Miranda,
and she's got this expression that's like,
Whoa! Thin ice here, thin ice!
So I say, Ah, therapy, and jump in
and tell my story about the therapist
my first wife and I saw
when it got to where we couldn't
stand each other anymore
and whose idea of a trust-building
exercise was for one of us
to blindfold the other
and lead that person around the mall,

a truly appealing opportunity
if you consider how humiliating
it would have been for me to run into
one of my students (neither "Dr. Dave,
is that you!" or "Who's the woman
in the blindfold, Dr. Dave?" held
any special appeal for me) and
therefore one that soon had
my then-wife and me laughing so hard
that for a brief time

        we forgot about the problems
that, of course, eventually
      caught up with us,

                  though who is to say
it was for the worse,
            since the failure
of that marriage made it possible
                  for me to meet, court, and marry
the woman I love now
            and in whose company
I am desperately trying
                  to salvage the evening by telling
an excruciating story on myself
            so that I won't have to listen
to an even more shameful
            one from someone else.

                  Therapy! It's best kept to one's self,
is it not, for it is reasonable,
            is moderate, is therefore
embarrassingly inadequate
                  when put up against the now-dead passion
it is meant to revive.
            Earlier that same week I'd had lunch
with a friend who'd told me he and his wife
                  were driving south to spend the weekend
in a little fishing village
            when suddenly his wife said, Oh, damn,
and he said, What?
            ʹand she said, I forgot my diaphragm,

                  and he said, Hold on,
I'll get some condoms,
            and he pulled into a convenience store
and surveyed the offerings
                  and came out and said,
Okay, they have A Hint of Mint,
            Super Safe with Nonoxynol-9,
Extra Ribs for Her Pleasure, and. . . .

Get the ribs, she said, and he said,
Hold on, there are four more choices,
        and she said, No, get the ribs,
I want the ribs,
        and I said, Right, that's how love should be,

        and another guy at the table,
an art historian by trade,
        was so encouraged by my enthusiasm
that he decided to tell his story,
        which is that he and his wife
had gone out and had a great meal
        and a bottle of Puligny Montrachet
and when they got home,
        they started making out
in the garden, and he was checking out
        his wife's breasts in the moonlight
and just about losing his mind,
        and then she knelt and unzipped his pants,

        and he said, Wait,
let me go in and get a blanket,
        and they ended up doing it in the yard
with her on top,
        and as he lay on his back
and looked at the night sky
        he remembered a saying
he'd seen on an old German engraving
        in the Prints Room
of the British Museum: *Nox et amor*
        vinumque nihil moderabile suadent,
or Night and love and wine
        urge nothing moderate,

        and I thought, Yes, yes,
that's how love should be,
        all wild and a little artistic, sure,
but mainly just crazy,
        like Prom Night, when David Neer
put his tongue in Kelly Holmes' mouth

and she fainted just dead away, pow,
like St. Teresa, only in Baton Rouge.
            Back in the restaurant, Miranda says,
Will you look at the time!
       so I signal the waiter for the check,
because there really is no reason
            to tell our dinner companions

                  that a few months after
my first wife and I had tried
            to get our derailed marriage
back on track and were now
                  looking at the double unhappiness
of the failed relationship
            and the failed sex therapy to boot,
I read in the paper one morning
                  that our therapist had sailed
a little boat out into Shell Point Sound
            and shot himself in the temple
with a short-barrelled .38, and I thought,
            Honestly, reason can kill you.

The Big Jacket

The French soldiers are stooping and circling
    each other with their hands behind their backs
à la Groucho Marx—it's La Scala, and the opera
    is Donizetti's *La Fille du Régiment,* but the set
is, first, an Alpine range like something you'd see

in an Ed Wood movie, with painted-on goats
    and mountains that threaten to topple whenever
a careless peasant bumps into one, and then,
    after the fille has left the régiment
for her doomed attempt to enter polite society,

a palace interior that resembles a frame
    in an R. Crumb comic with its lozenges
and furbelows and doohickeys and garish colors
    and exaggerated brush strokes. I love it.
And the singers! Over the top, everyone of them,

from the cowgirl fille, with her loping stride
    and tomboy mannerisms, to Tonio, her lover,
to the old duchess played by a man who,
    when the fille gets tangled up in her ball gown
and falls over backwards, says,

in his/her gravelly voice, "Elle est tombée"
    in a manner so flat and dry that everybody
in the audience cackles like guinea hens,
    including a formidable bunch of old blue-haired dames
in the orchestra seats who, come to think of it,

look as though they themselves might be men,
    might be their own husbands, as it were,
and so diverting is this opera,
    so much a divertissement is it,
that it is not until intermission

that I think back a month earlier
    and remember how irritated I was

when my credit card company called from Ohio
    to say someone in Italy wants to charge merchandise
to your account in the amount of 230,000 dollars,

and I say, It's not dollars, it's liras,
    and the guy says, Oh, it's not the same as dollars
over there? and I say—and I know I shouldn't
    say this, because even as I speak,
from the direction of Baton Rouge, LA

I feel my sleeping 94-year-old mother
    twitch in her armchair and grimace toward the east—
I say, Look, if having sex
    with farm animals makes you
so obtuse, why do you continue to do it?

which makes him so mad he puts his supervisor on,
    and she says, You have to understand,
the charge came from Italy,
    and here you are still in the states,
and I say, Listen, have you ever ordered something

from Williams-Sonoma, like, a wok or something?
    and she says, Sure, everybody's ordered something
from Williams-Sonoma, and I say, So what did you do,
    tell everybody in Columbus goodbye and then walk
to St. Louis and Boulder and Provo, and finally

you get to San Francisco, and you go to Williams-Sonoma
    and you get your wok, and then you walk all the way home,
and everybody back in Columbus says,
    Oh, hi, Marge, where you been?
and you say, Oh, well, had to go San Francisco,

had to get my wok, dontcha know? I mean, does it not
    seem possible that somebody could be in one place
and pick up the phone and order something
    from another place without actually being there?
And by this time she, too, has had it up to here

but has no superior to pass me on to,
    so she says, Such a gentlemen! and hangs up
just as I'm shouting, If you're not going to accept
    the charges, what I want to know is,
am I or am I not going to get my goddamn opera tickets?

and only then does it occur to me:
    what if they really have started to use dollars
in Italy and a cup of coffee now costs, you know,
    1500 dollars instead of 1500 liras?
But no, we go to the La Scala ticket office

the day of the performance and, sure enough,
    there are the tickets, and for good seats, too,
and we're so happy that we go to a café
    for a drink to celebrate, which is when Barbara
notices the tickets say "gentlemen are kindly requested

to wear jacket and tie," and I say,
    What does that mean, "kindly requested,"
and she says, It means if you don't satisfy
    the dress code, you might be kindly requested
to kindly not attend. So I ask Michele,

the night man at the hotel, if he has a jacket
    I can borrow, but it's a double-breasted jacket,
and Michele has a good eighty pounds on me,
    so when I put it on, I disappear.
Not that it matters once we're there,

where one of the best parts is that
    I am looking down into the orchestra pit
and for the first time can see
    how like a little city it is,
with the various craftsmen pursuing their trades

but also talking to each other and taking little breaks
    and even naps from time to time
and showing off their different personalities

as well, as is the case
with the young romantic cellist who,

alone among the older, staid,
    more civil-servant-type cellists,
is weaving back and forth
    and tossing his bushy hairdo
and arching his eyebrows and sighing

the way he knew he would when he was fourteen
    and already the best cellist in Gubbio or Pongibonsi
and dreaming of soloing under the baton
    of Zubin Mehta or Pierre Boulez at the Met
or the Royal Albert, so that even though

he's only part of an ensemble and an invisible one
    at that, he's happy to saw away
and fling his hair about and moan softly to himself,
    even though probably he knows one day
he'll be a geezer too, all of whom

had the same dream he did, but so what,
    tell anybody you're in the orchestra
at La Scala and they'll say, Oh, wow.
    And then there's the oboist
who works on his instrument constantly:

tightening one fitting, loosening another,
    reshaping a reed until there is nothing left
and then discarding it and beginning again
    as his colleagues look on
with what appears to be genuine interest,

although I have to imagine that at least
    some of them are thinking,
If Sergio doesn't stick that fucking thing
    in his mouth and start playing it,
I'm going to break it over his head,

and on stage the French soldiers are prissing around,
    and la fille is breaking their hearts left and right,
and Tonio the tenor escapes death by firing squad
    and gets la fille into the bargain—molto bravo!—
and I am so happy that I forget my jet lag

and my quarrels with the credit card company
    and even the big jacket I am wearing, all of which
makes a kind of sense, a gestalt, as it were,
    though no more than what you might expect
from the seemingly random events of a dream

or of our lives, which themselves
    are short, happy dreams, and we always try
to figure out our dreams, don't we?
    If we can remember them, that is.
This jacket is so big that I could have smuggled

a couple of additional opera lovers into
    La Scala with me the way we used
to hide guys in the trunks of our cars
    along with the beer and the Cheetos
when we went to the drive-in back in Baton Rouge.

And as we are walking back to the hotel,
    when Barbara says, "Look! There's Tonio!"
and of course it's not Tonio at all
    but the tenor who sings his part,
only now he's wearing street clothes

instead of his stage costume,
    just at that moment
I am wondering half seriously and half in fun,
    What if I open next year's fashion mags to see
headlines like "Big Jackets Are IT!"

and "If You Only Buy One Thing This Season,
    Make Sure It's A Big Jacket,"
but then I hear Barbara say, Look, there he is,

and I whirl around to cry "Bravo, signore!"
only I do a complete one eighty,

and the jacket keeps facing forward,
    and as I grin at him foolishly over the collar,
the guy who played Tonio looks at me like,
    first, What the hell, and then,
Does he have a gun in there,

so I hold out my hands to show
    I have only the best intentions,
and his face opens a little,
    and he's probably thinking,
Jeez, that's a big jacket,

and I'm definitely thinking,
    Gun? I could put the whole régiment
in this thing and la fille, too,
    because, let's face it,
the big jacket covers us all.

W. C. Rice's Cross Garden

We drive down to Prattville,
stopping first in Pink Lily
    to see Charlie "The Tin Man" Lucas
and the dinosaurs he makes out of car parts
    and sticks in his front yard and hangs in trees,
and the thing that strikes me about Mr. Lucas
  is that there appears to be no seam
between his art and his life,
    none of that irritable I-should-be-doing-
something-instead-of-talking-to-you feeling
  you sometimes get from artists, because obviously
he'd made dinosaurs all morning and would again
    that afternoon, and he treats our visit
as though it were a chance maybe to sharpen
    his focus a little or forget for a while
some problem he'll solve in the blink of an eye
    once he gets back to work,

    and over in Prattville,
W. C. Rice is pretty much the same way,
    not so much moving effortlessly
between art and life as not really recognizing
    that the two are different,
because, in his case, at least, they aren't.
  I am a lot more nervous about meeting him, though:
for one thing, it's later in the day,
    and there has always been something sad to me
about Sunday afternoons, which, when I was a child,
  were sandwiched between the fulminations
of Irish Catholic priests who out-Calvined Calvin
    and that sickly early-evening realization that
(a) next day was a school day with four more
    right after it and (b) I hadn't done my homework.
Too, you don't drive up to W. C. Rice's house
    past fields of big happy stegosauruses;

    instead, hundreds and hundreds
of rusted-out refrigerators and washer/dryer

combos and air-conditioner housings
are covered with crosses and slogans like
     NO DRINKING ALOUD and I THANK JESUS
FOR SAVING MY MOMMA AND DADDY and lots of
  variations on HELL IS A REAL PLACE
and HOT HOT HOT IN HELL and especially MEN IN HELL
     FROM SEX, which I see more than once.
So by the time Barbara and I are standing
  in front of W. C. Rice's door and I have raised
my hand to knock, the lapsed-Catholic part of me
     is ready to head back down the hill,
because I think, What if this fire-breathing
     holy roller decides we're laughing at him
and pulls a gun on us or simply bolts all the doors
     and windows and bores us to death,

     but it's too late, because just then
the door opens and we are invited in
     by Mr. Rice himself, who turns out to be
a plump little guy with a goatee
     who is well along in years and rather sickly
though sweet-natured and friendly
  if—not evangelistic, by any means,
but just the slightest bit pushy.
     For instance, he says, "Think about that" a lot,
even when he's talking about things we'd said,
  not him: "There's only one cross garden," he tells us,
"God didn't need two. Think about that.
     You look in the Bible, there's only one of everything.
Adam, one. Noah, one. Jesus, one. Of course
     the old king did put three in the fiery furnace. . . ." Me:
"But he only did it once." W. C. Rice: "That's right,
     he only did it once. Think about that."

     So we talk for a while
and think about everything a couple of times,
     and he signs some prayer cards for us,
and Barbara asks him
     if he is still adding to the cross garden,
and he says he has pretty much filled

his property and these days it's all he can do
        to keep up with the replacements,
because the frat boys from Troy State
    get ripped on Budweiser and hormones
and tear through from time to time and steal a few pieces
        for their girlfriends or the dorm room,
and I ask if it would be all right
            if we looked around a little more
before we go, and he says sure,
        take your time, come back when you can.

        So Barbara goes off in one direction
and I in another, and by this time
        the sun is low in the sky,
although it still lights the tops of the pines
        so brightly they redden like torches,
while around the trunks the darkness
    is thick and twisted and black,
and I think how Willy Loman's brother would say,
        The jungle is dark, Willy, but it's full of diamonds,
though I sure don't see any,
    and that's when I realize I have run out
of cross garden, that I am on the little dirt path
        that divides W. C. Rice's holy field
from the one place the devil would pick
        to sit and chew his liver and think,
Sooner or later some dumb shit
        is going to cross that road.

        I turn and see Barbara up by W. C.'s house,
and she waves at me, and I take a step,
        and just then a wind right out of January
almost knocks me over, only this is April,
        and by this time I am running
the way someone does when he's pretty sure
    that a big claw is reaching out
to pull the skin off his back
        and drag him into the woods and beat him
against the trees like a bloody dishtowel.
    I am running so hard, when I get to Barbara,

119

I do a couple of laps around her before I can stop.
   "Jesus, what's with you," she says, though I can't
explain it until we get back on the highway to Dothan,
   and after we get home and I find
I still can't get the terror out of my mind,
   I figure I'll write W. C. Rice about it,

    so in my letter I thank him and then ask
if there was something in those woods
   he had seen and I had only felt,
which is not all that crazy a thing
   to ask someone like W. C. Rice, because he'd told us
that he brought his father a Bible as he lay dying,
 and even though his daddy was in a coma,
W. C. opened up the Bible and put it
   by his daddy's bedside and stuck his head into the hall
to look for the nurse and when he turned around,
 his father was still lying there,
and there was nobody in the room
   and no way for anybody to get past,
but the Bible was closed, "and who
   do you think closed that Bible?"
Me: "The devil?" W. C. Rice:
   "That's right, the devil. Think about that."

   So I know he believes in a devil in a physical form,
and I convince myself that if he ever writes me back
   he'll say something like Yeah, I saw this thing
running low to the ground once and it had four heads
   and they were all biting at one another,
but when he does answer my letter, he says,
 No, there's nothing in those woods
that he knows of and that he'd made his cross garden
   because he had been born again into Christ Jesus,
and while he doesn't come out and say I'm crazy,
 I do feel a little screwy as I sit there and think, Hmmm,
here I am going hog wild on the dramatic possibilities
   while W. C. Rice, who sits around painting
MEN IN HELL FROM SEX on rusted-out gas ranges
   and old Chevys, is just taking care

of his spiritual bookkeeping, tidying up the ledger
        as calmly as an accountant would.

        Now he does say in his letter that if I want
to know more I should read Luke 16:16-31,
        which is the story of the rich man
who gave nothing to the beggar outside his gate,
        and when they both died, the rich man saw Abraham
afar off, and the beggar was in his bosom,
 and the rich man cried out in his agony,
but Abraham said, Between us and you
        there is a great gulf fixed, and that forever.
And about the time I get the letter
 I have been reading in the newspapers
about the Gilmore family and its
        most famous son, Gary, the killer,
and all this rolls around in my mind—the cross garden,
        my terror that day, the mild-as-milk life
of W. C. Rice and the art that blazed in the middle of it,
        the story Luke told of the rich man,

        and the story of the Gilmores, too, of the father
who beat Gary and the other boys every day of his life
        and who, if there is a hell (and there is,
Mr. Rice assures me once again in his letter),
        deserves to burn there.
But I don't believe in a hell like that—
 I'd lost my religion long ago,
and the farther I get from it,
        the more it seems to me that hell
isn't a big smoldering garbage dump
 like the one you see in the *New Yorker* cartoons
but another place altogether,
        one both subtler and more terrible
and also a place we are far more likely
        to find ourselves in on earth before we die
than after, with a great gulf fixed between us
        and everything we ever desired, the awareness

of which motivates just about everything we do,
for good or evil, a chasm that Charlie "The Tin Man" Lucas
      and W. C. Rice cross every time they make
a brontosaurus out of a John Deere tractor or paint I THANK
        THE LORD FOR SAVING MY DADDY on the side of a
freezer, but it's also a gap Gary Gilmore's father crossed
  whenever he took a tire iron to his children
if they'd been picked up by the cops
      or made the honor roll, it didn't matter,
and that Gary crossed, too,
  when he made those Mormon boys lie on the ground
and shot them in the head,
      and it's a gulf I crossed that afternoon
in Prattville as the trees flamed around me
      and I felt the woods reaching
and I looked up and saw Barbara on the hill
      and ran toward her and ran and ran.

My Twentieth Century

Madame greets us with a complimentary apéritif
and later pours a good half a cup of calvados
    on my meringue glacée before saying
Attendez, je vous flambe
    or hold on a sec, I'll flame you—

how droll the French are!—
but hey, I'm flaming already
    what with all this as well as the wine
I've drunk and the meal I've eaten with such esprit,
    seeing as how the clock is ticking

and I'm not sure I can say with any confidence
that I'll be back here before the century turns,
    but who's thinking about that right now,
because I am also sitting at my favorite table
    looking at the church of St. Étienne du Mont

and also at my wife's pretty American face
in the light of the candle
    that gutters gently in the almost too-chilly wind
as we finish dessert and Madame brings us
    a free snort of brandy and then,

to my astonishment, but who am I to refuse,
a free glass of champagne after that,
    during which I am telling Madame,
You know, Madame, I always come here
    on my first night in Paris, and she says,

I know, and I say, You know? and she says,
Certainement, monsieur, what do you think
    the free drinks are for, and the next thing
I remember is that we are walking around
    the Jardin du Luxembourg and it is as though

my body has been cut in half, with my head
and heart in full command of the intellect
    and the emotions even as my legs and feet

seem to have taken on a life of their own
     and are trying to get away from the rest of me

     like a bad dog that wants to run ahead
and sniff the bushes and snap at other dogs,
     and the cars are trying not to hit it,
and they're crashing into one another
     and flipping and burning and running up

     onto the sidewalk and smashing the fruit stalls
and knocking over the hydrants
     so the water is gushing everywhere,
and the old ladies are crying Mon dieu, Mon dieu,
     while the dog's master is trying both

     to call it back and also to look indignant
for the sake of passersby, as if to say,
     Though my dog is a very bad animal indeed,
you can see by my indignation, dear sir
     or madame, that I, like you, am a person

     of breeding and restraint who is trying
to do his best with a creature
     completely lacking in both qualities,
and I try to explain all this to Barbara
     secretly, that is, in French, until I remember

     that we are in France, and while what I am saying
would likely remain a secret were we walking
     down the streets of our own dear small town
of Tallahassee, Florida, here it would be
     crystal clear to Marcel and Pierre and Sophie,

     so I give up on that part, and meanwhile
this bad dog of mine keeps trying
     to entangle itself in the limbs
of other French people, I mean, French people
     who are simply waiting to cross the street

     or are otherwise minding their business,
and before I realize what I am saying, I say,

Stop that this instant, César!
and I think, yes, I will call that part
   of me that has turned into a bad dog

César and try to keep it in check
by admonishing it in the severest terms
   when it disobeys me and perhaps even give it
a spirited caning if it continues
   to swivel this way and that and go left

when I have distinctly ordered it to go right
and to stumble over curbs when I have warned it
   repeatedly that curbs are approaching
and to pester other people when I have
   ordered it to keep its distance.

I sure do like the French.
Contrary to stereotype, they are
   a most amiable people: quick with courtesy,
generous with everything they have,
   and kind to animals, even bringing their dogs

with them to restaurants, though not bad dogs
like César. A Parisian would have no use
   for a dog like this, and I myself put up
with him only because he is my dog
   and also because there are moments

when a vicious cur like César
would be a most delectable companion,
   and when I say this I am thinking
of this afternoon when we were in
   the Musée d'Orsay, which, like all museums,

has signs that say "NO FLASH!"
in several languages and include
   the little ideogram of the flash going off
with the circle around it and a stripe
   through it for the illiterate,

meaning,in fact, everyone except
the three or four thousand selfish ignoramuses
     every goddamned day who figure,
No, sir, doesn't apply to me,
   I didn't get where I am today by following the rules,

     plus my kid could have painted half this crap anyway,
so why shouldn't I take my snaps
     instead of buying the cards in the shop downstairs
where they'll probably cheat me,
     seeing as how I don't know the language and all,

     so they haul out their Instamatics,
as this one woman did in the Orsay there,
     propping up her shovel-faced husband in front
of Pierre-Auguste Renoir's *Le Moulin du Bal
de la Galette* and firing away, the guy

     looking like one of those
dead horse thieves they photographed
     in their coffins in the frontier towns
as a lesson to others, just lifeless,
     like, What a bunch of crap, I didn't want

     to come here anyway, I'd rather be on line,
and his wife is flashing away,
     and you can almost hear the paint scream,
the chips flying off the canvas
     and out into the Paris afternoon

     the way the calendar pages would fly off the wall
in those old Warner Brothers movies
     so you'd know time was passing,
and as I stumble through the Paris night,
     trying to get my bad dog under control,

   I think, You want screams? I got screams for you!
Get 'em, César! Bite the guy's leg! Strip 'em naked,
     both of them! Now get the camera, boy!
That's it, take the film out!
     Yeah, run around with it in your mouth—

expose that sucker!
And the woman would scream and beg
    for her clothes back. And Zombie Boy
would come to life and let out a "melancholy, long,
  withdrawing roar" like the one Matthew Arnold

    heard on Dover Beach. And the century
would come to a close—my twentieth century!
    Mine and César's. There were good dogs
and bad dogs in it, Gandhis and Hitlers.
    When Hitler said You French there,

    you give up toot sweet, they more or less
replied Oui, oui. But it turns out they were right:
    zuh beautiful city she is spared;
zuh Fascist monstair, he is leesen more
  to hees astrologues zan to hees generals;

    zuh war, she is poof; and zuh victory,
she is ours. Now it's time
    to go through customs again, the way we do
every hundred years. And you bet
  we've got something to declare:

    we've got good stuff, we've got bad stuff,
and *sans doute* we've got weird stuff,
    the kind of things you can't explain
but turn out to be what you wanted
  in the first place, even though

    you didn't know it at the time.
By now I am not sure what part of Paris
    we are in because we are wandering around
like the men in De Soto's expedition through
  what is now the southeastern United States,

    doubling back on their old steps and retracing
paths they had already trod upon and thinking,
    as one of them wrote in his journal,
that only when he died and looked down from heaven
  would he be able to make sense of his roving

here on earth, and then I think:
how uncanny it would be to look down on
      my twentieth century that way!
To see my mother riding a horse to school,
      my teenaged father weeping as his parents die

      and then going off to school in Heidelberg
while the Brown Shirts marched and people wondered,
      You think there's going to be a war?
Then them getting married and having my brother
      and me, and my father carrying me

      into the hospital, afraid to speak
because he thought I might have polio,
      which I did, and them getting older
and dying and me growing up
      and marrying and having kids and divorcing

      and re-marrying and feeling smart some days
and stupid others but mainly doing
      the best I can, putting my life together
the way the century itself
      is assembled, i. e., bit by bit.

Or is it bite by bite? And isn't that our hotel?
And wasn't that a tremor? Yes to all three.
      The century is coming to its feet
as we slide from its lap—woof, woof!
      Old friend, where are you going in your cardigan,

      your baggy pants? Ah, I see: into history,
where no one will understand you.
      You shuffle down the Boul' Mich'—wait!
Take my dog César; he'll protect you!
      There they go, the two of them, to the métro.